FOUR CORNERS
OF THE CIRCLE

There is difference between "First Move" and "Move First". Concentrate on your First Move, it is always an advantage.

M. J.

FOUR CORNERS
OF THE CIRCLE

MOHIT JAIN
WITH
AMITA SOOD

PARTRIDGE
A Penguin Random House Company

Logos designed at MJ Magic Studio by Jyoti Ahirwar and Dipanwita Bag

To order additional copies of this book, contact
Partridge India
000 800 10062 62
www.partridgepublishing.com/india
orders.india@partridgepublishing.com

Thanks to my dreams which had never allowed me to sleep,
and thanks to all who had never seen me sleeping.

CONTENTS

PROLOGUE

I always have had problems with designs. May be, this is the reason that my beloved students and friends teasingly call my problems as "designer problems".

It simply does not mean that I have problems with designers (machine designers, model designers or dress designers) but yes, I have problems with designs. The way few assumptions are embedded in them, the way the operators play with the assumptions, the way people make mockery of these designs and still never step ahead and change them.

Let us take for an instance my own case, I always wanted to change these designs so that they fit best as per the scenario and changing demands. Though the creators might not have any problem with me altering the set of assumptions, the followers of these designs have always raised questions about my faithful intentions to change the designs.

In the end, I often ask myself, what am I, who am I? I am a Management Consultant. A consultant whose job is to transfer the decisions taken by top management and funnel them down to junior levels who feel proud to implement them assuming solutions are provided by me, an outsider to the company. My job was to transcript, embed and augment their solutions in such a manner that it looks like as if I invented them.

We need to take a closer look at the design of the management team. Here the lower level doesn't want to look upon the advice of their seniors but are always ready to accept and follow whatever is asked by some unknown outsiders, who claim themselves as "Management Consultants". Bitter but true, asked many times, am I a management consultant, or just a puppet in hands of the design?

The question hounds me again and again. Who I am? I am a speaker. Once being applauded for my speech during my post graduation days and claimed as an upcoming speaker in the days to come; I proclaimed myself to be a speaker and started speaking on any topics of concern. The irony was that many a times I found myself in company of those who acknowledge themselves as my listeners. I often ask myself, are they really my good listeners or am I helping them out with their some unknown purpose? Guess what! I was right this time. Many of them were there to attend to my oration, keeping in mind their range of superior knowledge. They would only look at the subject with critical analysis. They wanted to portray my points as wrong. We need to check the design of a successful speech. We start with the issues not addressed or poorly addressed by others, so that we can attract more audiences. Have we ever started a speech with our strengths? A bit afraid, here I am in quoting this, never. We have never started with our strengths.

So now I need to wonder if there is a flaw in the mass's opportunistic outlook or some thing wrong in the design of the 'speaker' that I am. Am I designed to speak the things am speaking or just following another design?

I am a trainer. I can still recollect the very first assignment I did as a trainer. Got a call from the organizers and e-mailed them my training modules for 6 hours, starting 2 hours of Nine Point Theory©, followed by two group games of one hour each and then two hours on Virtual Imaging©. "We don't care what you will take up during those six hours. What we really care is, at the end of the session, either they all are in the organization working seriously or each one of them simply end up submitting their resignations. Either they are in or simply out of the system. Be simple or arrogant; master it or be tamed; but we need results by 6 o'clock." and bang it goes the call. I was still glaring at my handset with mouth wide open. This was the first and last briefing by my organizers. Before the inglorious session, the leading lady from the organizers came up to me and said, Look! These Fellas think they know everything which exists and does not exists in this world. Your job is to make them realize that reality is exactly the other side of the coin, which they had never seen before. I raised my doubt, the famous one!, again regarding the design of the training structure as a whole. When they know everything, are they going to listen to me? Moreover, if the company wants to retrench them, why is The Company not doing it by its own? Answers, as if, were known to me, still I asked. Simple, no one wants to take the blame on themselves. So, Who I am? A trainer or an angel of death! A human or a machine, scheduled to work as per the design?

An educationalist can take form of a teacher, instructor, lecturer, professor, tutor, guru, coach or a mentor. Post graduate students used to call me their mentor. The best part is that till now the meaning of this word is lying in the "Paradigm Shift" mode and still I pronounce myself as a mentor, because they call me one.

I am a Mentor. On the day of induction of new batch, I receive a list which consists of the names of the students for whom I need to play the role of a mentor. A day was also assigned for our weekly meet. I don't remember for how many weeks we actually met in full quorum. At the end of the session, I saw her for the first time in mentor meet. "I guess young lady, you are in the wrong meet", I announced. "Sorry Sir, I couldn't make out these days as I was tied up with all project works and extracurricular activities and was also doing some PR activities on behalf of the college", here comes the excuse from the fairer end. After a fair long discussion, the motive of all being present in the meet comes alive—It was time for mentor's approval on their project reports. In spite of the fact that none of the reports were up to the mark I still gave my comments and approval for all except one. As expected, the smiling face an hour ago wasn't delightful the way it was but was still smiling as if it was warning me about something. Eyes were staring at me, indicating that something was there, something which was enigmatic and mysterious. No voice raised, she left the meet, while rest of the group was busy with their thanks giving activity.

"Director Sir is calling you immediately to his chamber", announces the peon piping in my faculty room, just after ten minutes, I called off the meet. "Sign on her report and let her go. She being busy with our college work itself, we promised her that she will get a clear approval on her project, if she works with us", hearing this straight from the horse's mouth shocked me for a while. Design again surrounded me by never ending queries. Is this what a mentor is supposed to do! A correct word wrongly placed, or a wrong word correctly placed. It should be rather "Mentoy©", a person meant to be used as a toy in hands of a design; a design which runs an institute.

I used to type articles from the newspaper just to improve my typing speed. So you can imagine what my typing speed would be! But wait, that set of typing day in and day out was not for increasing my speed of typing, but just to hide myself from myself. Days when I used to have no work and needed to sit back at home doing nothing, I used to type just to show that I am working. As a result, people started calling me a writer.

I am a writer. During my non working hours, I started writing and/or typing data, numbers, and theories; hence became a content writer. Once a publisher asked me to show my work on a particular subject, which is also supposed to be very near to my heart. "Can you frame something like this?" publisher raised a question and I answered; "Can't we have something out of the content I already have and over that I will also follow the same sequence, while I teach." 'Look, Mohit Sir, we also want this book to be sold in the market. If you can design the book on these lines, then we will give you three four more books, from where you can assemble the content and we will have a book which can be sold readily in the market'.

I wrote whatever was being asked. I delivered it on time and the book got published but with reference to some well known established author. I got space only in the third line of the last paragraph of the acknowledgements section. Next year, new edition and my name got replaced by some other writer. This is the design of the writing world. I don't think I am a good writer, but yes publisher had sold more than 30,000 copies of that write up and they claim that it is all because of the "design'. I was a ghost writer, with no existence of his own, and supposed to work on the pre-set designs again.

Hearing my friend reciting a lovely piece of poetry over the lunch break, I thought of writing poems too. It was 1992, and I knew nothing about the art of "poetry". I started rhyming and take words from the poetry of renowned poets. I am a poet and truly speaking, I don't have any problems being one, as I had never followed any designs here. It has been more than 20 years now and I have tried writing different styles of poetry in all these years. "But sir, you have to listen to us also, we can't publish this, as there is no design. You have to follow certain rules and write according to our designs". I have been hearing this from last ten years. I never believed in following designs or patterns created by them and hence I have no buyers for my poems. That is who I am. A poet without design and hence no audiences!

I am a teacher. This is what I am! A teacher fighting for a change in designs!

You may ask, why I haven't said anything on my role as a teacher. It's not that I am satisfied with the designs here, but yes I need to say something, rather many things on my role as a teacher.

This book is about the journey of a man and the lessons he gets from his 16 years of teaching career. Throughout our lives, we keep on moving in circles and still search for the corners knowing that there are no corners in the circle. We rest for a while and then again begin our journey on the never ending circular path.

In all these years, I have had many bitter and sweet experiences which had taught me priceless lessons of life. Moving in circles, I finally discovered the mantra of success which helped me to cross all hurdles of life. The secret of success are embodied in 5 simple rules which form the fifth corner of the square.

If you dream of flying with eagles you cannot afford to swim with ducks. Every one of us wishes to achieve success, power and fame but fail to realise the hardships behind that triumph. You go out for a lunch not just to have good food but also to enjoy the company of your near and dear ones. The more you spend and the better restaurant you go, the more will you enjoy the ambiance, services and food.

Similarly, the more inputs you make the better will be your output. You can expect to have a placement in one of the top notch companies only if you have worked hard throughout the year.

Imagination, a very powerful word forms the basis of everything existent in this world. I often draw pictures in my mind and imagine the entire situation in my mind before it actually happens. The visualization of pros and cons of every decision that I take helps me to adjudicate what is right or wrong for me. Every time I used to go for an interview, I used to think of all possible questions that the interviewer could ask me. To my surprise, the interviewers really asked the questions that I thought about.

Imagine the virtual; something which does not exist. Expand your visions and turn your dreams in to a beautiful reality. Start visualising. You need to master the art of anticipating beyond your vision in order to achieve something which no one has so far, but with no catastrophic end.

Stop following the crowd. Instead of mimicking someone else's style why you don't be yourself and create your own fashion statement. When I say fashion, I do not just mean the way you dress but the way you think! If you think fashionably, only then will you be able to make your unique identity. Not only you need to be a trend setter but also learn to manage your style.

"Nine Point Theory©" is the concept which I have created in these 14 years and it might sound something very new. This theory helps you to identify who you are, what you want and how can you accomplish it. I explain this theory to my students before the session ends in order to bid a farewell to them by giving them some powerful thoughts and tools which could help them to become successful in their lives.

At the end, it is Hope on which the entire world is running. You end up losing everything but the only thing that keeps you going is "Hope".

The positive spirit inside you gives you the strength to look for the opportunities even in the darkness. To find a hope of victory in the lost world! The power to transform the darkness in to light with our knowledge!

Four Corners of the Circle is a small attempt in transforming the bounded class rooms back to era of open Gurukuls.

I have a long way to go!

I often ask myself;

Whom do we love the most in this beautiful life given to us?

Which eternal power kills our happiness and still says that everything in the world is immortal?

Who introduces us to truth and reality, makes us happy from the bottom of our heart?

Who tells us why to live, for whom to live and whom to die for?

Who is the one who keeps changing us?

Who has the plan to make us free from assumptions and designs?

Who has the key to give us wings to fly?

It is no one else but "Us"

We have everything what we want for ourselves!

We have the strength to face every challenge of life!

So let us strive for our own identity!

It is you! You have all the weapons that you need!

Now Fight!

ROUND 1

One should not do MBA

1

Educational Institutions

I have been training students for B. School entrance examinations for about 12 years now. In all these years, many students come up to me and ask:

Will they get admission in a reputable business school and what efforts do they require to make to be able to achieve their target?

My reply to their question is another question:

Why you want to pursue MBA? Here were some of the answers which baffled me.

- An MBA degree provides avenues for better job opportunities.
- My parents want me to study further.
- A post graduate degree is a must for financial success.

- The popularity of the MBA is following a rising trend.
- My friends have done it and they are quite successful.

If these are the primary factors initiating the interest among students in pursuing post graduation degrees then one should not do MBA.

My concern here is how many of these students are actually passionate about management and hold a strong desire to be versed with each of its aspects in depth.

This is our denunciation of profitable management institutions who have converted the pure virtue of education into a mere business.

If we see the graph of number of MBA colleges in India, we observe a positive trend from 2006-07. There is consistent growth during the period 2008-10. However, this growth comes to a halt when we move towards 2012-13. [Source: AICTE]

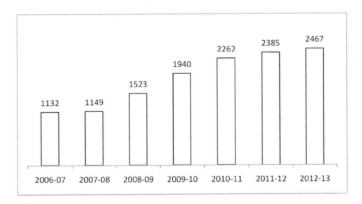

Who is responsible for the current situation of management industry?

Are students or educational institutions solely to be blamed for this degradation?

No. My argument is neither directed towards students nor educational institutions. I oppose everyone who does not understand the actual purpose of post graduation courses like MBA.

Previously, only a handful of people understood the true value of education as a result of which the count of MBA colleges was unsubstantial.

When India opened its arms to the world of technology, a sudden rise in the educational institutions was observed. Several promising Business Schools came up offering attractive course curriculum and placement services.

Sadly, at the end of the course, those promises remained unfulfilled which created resentment among students who had very high expectations from their college.

The reason behind this is that the agenda of the colleges has been shifted from growth of the students to financial profit. This has further led to retrogression of these profitable MBA colleges.

Being in the teaching industry for several years, I have had acquaintance with several business schools titleholders who frequently make an appeal to promote their institution so that they could fetch the maximum number of students and hence the maximum amount of profit.

A genuine institution never feels the need to ask for recommendations. If the quality of education that they provide is good then their results speak for themselves. Students automatically provide positive feedback about the institution and refer their near ones to join it as well.

Only if they are missing out on something; they ask others to recommend them.

Have you ever observed that the most popular brand among the common people are often least advertised?

People feel the need to spend an extra amount of money on promotion only if the sale of their product or service is below a satisfactory level.

Nowadays, it is possible to launch a business school even with a little investment. These institutions leave no stone unturned to promote themselves. Be it newspaper advertisements or be it online marketing, they try their level best to get maximum attention from the students.

They endorse their colleges by ensuring best faculty, excellent facilities and state of the art infrastructure which could help in the transformation of the students into successful entrepreneurs.

But

How many colleges actually fulfil these promises?

Students have become nothing but their source of income and the sole purpose of establishing these educational institutes has become profit making business.

If the only purpose of educational institutes is to make huge profits then **one should not do MBA.**

These profitable institutes take advantage of the fact that there is a cut throat competition in the Management industry today and the number of vacancies is very less as compared to the Management graduates. They tempt the students to join their college by showing that they have the best placement record and assuring a good job upon completion of the course.

If by chance any of their students excel in his/her career, the college highlights it for several years even if the complete credit of that student's success goes only to his/her own efforts.

Unfortunately, there are only a few colleges which concentrate on the quality of education which could help in building the future of the students.

Today, every 5 out of 10 graduates opt for MBA as a postgraduate degree without even knowing what it is all about. Some of them cannot even tell what its full form is.

The business people make use of this unawareness and influence them to join their college. Later, when the things do not happen as expected, students lose their faith in educational institutions.

Colleges follow a model of pedantic education which is not sufficient for overall growth of students as management executives. They need much more than good books and notes.

If at the end, students have to study from their text books only then what is the point of heavy fees paid to the college?

What they really need is **practical exposure**, **experience** and **knowledge** which cannot be imparted through books. Mentors should share their own priceless experiences with the students which would make them familiar with different aspects of the MBA. Not only a mentor has to provide in depth knowledge on the subject but also guide students how to implement them in real life.

Implementing the knowledge is as important as gaining it.

The sole purpose of educational institutions should be offering a great education for the better tomorrow. Rather than making efforts in selling their institutes, they should invest their time, money and energy in improving the quality of education.

They need to understand if they concentrate on providing finest quality education, rest will fall in place automatically. Then they would not need to go out of their way to promote their institutes.

The educational institutes should change their approach shifting their focus from doing business to providing good education.

"An investment in knowledge pays the best interest" ~ *Sir Benjamin Franklin*

Let us throw a light on the education in the past. The education has played a major role in the enlightenment of our country. Some of the most successful entrepreneurs of India like **Aditya Vikram Birla**, **Ratan Naval Tata**, **Adi Godrej** and **Azim Premji** have always given importance to education in their lives. The education provided them the courage and wisdom to bring revolution in the world of technology.

Where is the fire to succeed, curiosity to learn lost?

Today most people need a job only to be able to earn their living.

And if this is the reason, then one should not do MBA.

2

My Beloved Students

By following a correct approach, one can give a positive turn to his/her life. All we need to do is to make right decisions in our personal as well as professional lives.

But are students following a correct approach towards their career?

After completing graduation, youngsters get into the rage of getting a good job in a multinational company with a handsome package irrespective of the fact whether they studied during the entire course or not. They simply need a job which is not at all easy. Today, companies want to hire brightest students who are not only technically competent but also possess excellent communication skills and the right attitude.

Their real struggle begins once they pass out and step into the corporate world. After a point, they get frustrated and start looking for other alternatives.

When they do not get a job they feel that going for further studies is a good option but . . .

Are they really interested in pursuing higher education or is it just an escape from unending struggle, parental pressure and questions raised by people around them?

All the students who have chosen MBA should do self introspection and decide if they really want to do MBA or not. If they are doing it for any reason other than their own interest, they would end up being in a much messier situation.

At first instance, it sounds easy to pursue an MBA and then get high paid jobs but it is not as simple as students think. MBA involves 2 years of consistent hard work and devotion.

Once students decide to seek graduation in a particular stream, they are enthusiastic initially but as the course begins, they eventually lose their interest in studies because they focus shifts on other things like, watching movies, hanging around with friends and of course dating.

Only once the course is about to complete, they remind themselves that they need to study or they will not get a job.

Similarly, even if they aim for MBA, initially, it could be fascinating for them but at a later stage they might lose interest in that too. After 2 years, they will find themselves trapped in the same situation.

So, genuine interest and right approach should always be taken into consideration before making any decision in career.

It is a wrong notion that having a post graduation degree could add value to your career. There is a condition to it. Yes, a post graduation degree can add value to your career if and only if you have in depth knowledge of the subject at the end of the course. Otherwise, this degree is nothing but just another piece of paper.

If you have cleared your entrance examination for MBA, the next step is to get admission in a good business school.

What is the first thing that you will expect out of a good MBA college?

Let me guess. The first concern would be the placement services that a college offers. So, if a college promises excellent placement, you would blindly join it immediately. Colleges will set bait for the students using the sugar of good placement opportunities; and the students will be attracted and they are trapped for next two years.

We are so lost in the race of being rich and successful that we have actually forgotten the real essence of education.

Education is something which every student should treasure and not take it as a burden. Sadly, education has rather now created fear in the minds of students. The fear of rejection. The Fear of not being able to prove themselves in front of their parents and society. This could lead to emotional and mental trauma among the students.

Only experience could provide them confidence to be a successful entrepreneur or a skilled employee.

Now let us try a new formula. Switch your mantra from "Job and Money" to "Knowledge and Experience" and then see the difference.

Give your best and have faith than success will automatically follow suit.

If you really wish to focus on your studies then you need to stop caring about the end results. Thinking about the outcomes would distract you from your path. Take out this thought from your mind: **Will I be able to achieve what I want?** This would simply discourage you. Instead just keep your focus aligned on gaining thorough knowledge about your subjects and soon you would achieve your goals.

Now, a question that appears in the mind of every student is how to get extra ordinary results?

Here are few pointers that would help students in attaining good results:

- If you have a desire to learn, you can initiate reading books other than the ones which are a part of your course curriculum.
- Today, so much material is available online which could provide great knowledge about different subjects of MBA.
- Go through blogs, candidate experiences available on the internet in order to know the current position of the market.

- Do a detailed research on different opportunities available for you once your course is completed. Make pointers and decide what job role would suit your knowledge, skills and interests.
- Set one target. Be clear about what you want to do and focus only on that. Do not think that you will go where your luck takes you. Have a goal and work towards it.

This knowledge would give you an upper edge over students who simply own a degree but have no knowledge about this industry.

In the war between knowledge and degree, knowledge wins and will always win! Knowledge is a treasure which will be with you even if you lose all your riches. No one can take away your knowledge from you; it stays even in your worst times.

The need of the hour is to guide the students to be strong enough, to take their decisions according to what they feel and not to come under the influence of their friends, parents and peers.

They need to realize that they will never regret the decision which they have taken on their own because the desire in them will always motivate them to prove that their decision is correct.

One should not do MBA just because their friends or relatives are doing it. If you are instead good at cooking, trust me, go for it, you will never regret it.

Sit alone and think what one thing you are actually good at is?

Are you really interested in doing MBA?

If that moment, your heart says yes, go for it without a second thought.

3

A Bouquet of Offerings!

The students need to understand the difference between the placement agencies and MBA colleges. If the colleges are providing excellent placements for their students, consider it complimentary to good education. For example; If you go to market for purchasing your favourite smart phone; you get a charger, headphones, a data cable and a user's manual free of cost with it.

Now will you purchase a phone simply to get the headphones? No. Right?

If you simply want the complimentary items like head phones then you would rather go to a market and buy them directly instead of wasting valuable money on the phone.

Aren't you doing exactly the same thing by considering Business Schools as a substitute to Placement Agencies?

First of all, you need to concentrate on the two year course curriculum and give your best in understanding and implementing the core concepts of management. Then you can expect complimentary benefits like good placement, scholarship, free books or laptops.

The main purpose of the B. School is not to provide jobs to the Management students but to polish their skills and making the students aware of different aspects of management; a manager or an administrator needs.

If a good job is all you want, then you should hire a placement agency rather than paying huge amount of fee for post graduation degree courses like MBA.

It is simply a waste of time, energy and money. Students keep blaming B. Schools if they do not get the job after completion of the course but they need to think, are they actually capable of doing a Management job.

It is wrong on the part of the students to think that even if they don't study, they will get a good job because they are studying in a good college which offers good placement opportunities.

The only thing that could get them the job is their intellect and their knowledge.

Colleges provide facilities like scholarship, laptop, good food and great infrastructure with a motive of providing a healthy environment for the students which encourages learning and facilitates their growth.

The students should take all these facilities provided to them in a positive way. They need to take out the negativity from their mind that everything colleges do is only for their promotion. May be, the college administration wants to make sure that the students do not face any issues which could hamper their studies. This is because if the students are not feeling comfortable in the college, they might lose focus from their studies as well.

There are some students who perform very well once the session begins but gradually they lose interest because they aren't comfortable with the environment of the college. This is the reason why colleges attempt to provide the best facilities to the students like food, laptop and scholarship.

Not that every college provides facilities to sell their business and make it their marketing strategy. We should not misinterpret their efforts.

You should expect only what you deserve. Expecting a great job without having skill is like expecting a tree which is watered every day but is fruitless.

Students who do not know the simple ABC of their essential skills and knowledge should have no right to coax colleges if they do not get a placement. They need to first get their basics right before preparing for an interview. Some students will get formal clothes and shoes before going for an interview so that they can leave a good impression on the employer's mind. However, when asked they cannot even answer simple questions related to their subjects.

Can we really blame B. Schools for this?

Well, to some extent the business schools have a control over the interest of the students but the success and failure of the student largely depend on his own **Attitude.**

If a student has a desire to accomplish something then even if they are not provided best facilities, they will excel in their careers.

Even if they are not studying in the best college, they will become the shining star of the college and will have the strength to change the reputation of the college in a positive way, by proving themselves.

On the other hand, if the students want plum jobs without making any conscious efforts, then all they will get at the end is the disappointment. One needs to realize that their struggle does not end by getting an admission in a good college, the real fight starts once the course begins.

Here, I propose to bring back the JUICE of wisdom. Join us in creating education and help us to free the students from the barbed chains of society, family pressure or rising competition. Let us give wings to the dreams of aspiring youth of our country. Let us relish the education. Let us enjoy the learning. Let us keep the fire of knowledge alive.

Books don't discriminate. You can learn irrespective of who you are or what you are. Keep learning and you will feel that you still have a long way to go even at the age of 69!

ROUND 2

69 and I am Here

4

Life Without Numbers

I always wanted to be a typist. When I was in 6th standard, everyday my school bus dropped me at a stop nearby my house. As I walked towards my home after a day full of learning experiences, I observed several typists sitting in a small room moving their fingers rapidly on the typewriter. I wondered how amazing it is that they could quickly type whatever they want, without even looking at the keys. I was so fascinated by them that one fine day I told my mother, "I want to learn Typing!" My mother smiled looking at my small dreamy eyes and made me join type writing classes.

I was finally able to dance my fingers on the typewriter quickly without even looking at it. I felt delighted because after struggling for so many days I had competently mastered the art of Typing.

Since my childhood, I had always scrutinized things carefully and had a curiosity to learn them. The best part is, despite facing many hurdles; I was eventually able to achieve what I desired.

'Desire', a very powerful word which can drive you to win over anything that you actually want in your life!

I am sure most of you must have gone through *'Mathematics Phobia'* at some point of time in your life. Parents do not leave any stone unturned in order to perfect their children in the subject of Mathematics from the beginning of their school life; because one can excel in this subject only if he has a strong base. Most of you feel annoyed when your parents and teachers keep on insisting you to study Mathematics!

For me, it was just the opposite. Numbers attracted me from the beginning and my mother always stopped me from studying Mathematics continuously for hours without a break. She used to scold me saying, "*Close your books and go to sleep! You have to wake up early tomorrow for going to school!*" After being scolded I used to quickly slip onto my bed and think what is going to be my target for the next day. I used to be engrossed in my thoughts and slowly fall asleep.

My life is incomplete without numbers! Every day, I feel like playing with the magical numbers and discovering new Mathematical concepts. This curiosity gradually helped me in gaining expertise in this subject.

5

---

*Don't run away from your
problems, conquer them!*

After finishing my schooling, I took up subjects like Economics, Statistics and Financial Accounting because they involved mathematics. Most of you quit on a mathematical problem, if you are unable to resolve it even after making several attempts. I, on the contrary, believe in conquering my weaknesses by solving that problem. Even if I spend whole day thinking about that particular mathematical query I wouldn't mind. And the moment I solve it, I will have a sense of accomplishment which will give me infinite confidence.

My motto of life is **'Don't run away from your problems, instead conquer them'!**

Many students are disappointed because despite making constant efforts, they only get failure at hand. This discourages them and makes them think that they don't possess the intellect to clear such examinations. I believe that the problem is not with their intelligence or effort, the root cause of their failure is the **approach** that they follow. If they cram everything without understanding the depth of the concepts, they will not be able to have a strong command over the subject. Instead, if they solve just one problem but understand the concept thoroughly, they will be able to solve any problem given to them. Rather than hurrying up and trying to solve all the problems at once, you should spend time on one problem and try to solve it without taking any help from books or mentors. This will give you immense confidence and sharpen your brain.

Shaleen, my student was excellent at all the subjects related to Management. No one could defeat him when it came to confidence, communication skills, intellect, English and Management skills.

The only thing which he was scared of was Mathematics. His entire score would go down just because of this subject.

He was highly dissatisfied and had lost confidence on himself. Negative thoughts crept in his mind like, "I am not capable of doing this."

One day I asked him, "Why are you deteriorating so much? I expected you to score among the highest." With a disappointed face he said that "In spite of spending countless number of sleepless nights for preparation of the exam, my overall score is still low because of Mathematics. Even after trying my best I am still not able to perform up to the mark!"

To boost him up I told him that even I had faced such situations in my own life, when even after giving my best; my scores were far less as compared to what I had expected.

However, I did not let my low marks shirk my faith on myself. Instead, they ignited a fire inside me; fire to kill the problems which I wasn't able to solve.

My fight began with those particular mathematical problems and I made sure I will be the winner.

At last, I murdered them and then I shone like a diamond when it came to performance.

My dear; even you should follow the same in your life and it is certain that your performance will be flawless one day.

He smiled at me and thanked me for those motivational words. To my delight; in the final exams; he scored the highest in Mathematics and stood first in the class as he was already good at other subjects.

I believe we all have the capability to win in life if we kill our problems instead of getting scared of them.

6

Being Brutally Honest

On the first day of my MBA classes, our professor asked everyone sitting in the class *"For what purpose have you joined MBA?"* All the students came up with different answers. Some wanted to get a good job in the field of Management and some wanted to add a post graduation degree to their name.

When my turn came I affirmatively said *"I want to become a Management trainer and better than any other management faculty!"*

Everyone in the room was stunned at my guts to challenge the experienced faculty member on his face! They all turned back and gazed at me for a moment giving me the 'You are dead' and 'How dare you' look!

The professor who taught us the subject of operations was very much respected by all the students. There always would be a pin drop silence in his class. That power he owned! One fine day, I was struggling to understand 'Markov process' taught by him. I found the concept very complicated and confusing and until I felt satisfied that I clearly understood it; I didn't let him go further with his lecture. Every time he asked me *"Have you understood"*, I simply nodded my head saying *"No sir!"* He was finally annoyed with me saying that *"You are the only one who has problem with everything! I never had to repeat the same thing to the other students so many times!"*

My answer to his statement was ***"If I am not able to understand this concept then I am sure no one in the class does either!"***

I have never been afraid to call a spade a Spade and express what I feel. I believe being brutally honest is always better than giving someone fake appreciation. Till date, I have never regretted speaking the truth. Even if it creates several problems for me in the initial phase of my personal as well as professional life; the end result was always beautiful. I lost many things because of being direct and honest which pinched me at some point in my life. However, I realised whoever and whatever is still there with me is actually mine!

7

Roll Number 32

When the results were being announced by the same professor, he moved to roll number 33 without declaring the result for roll number 32. I politely asked him "*Sir, could you please tell me the scores for roll number 32?*" He called me and said with a smile on his face "*Roll number 32 has scored 100 marks!*"

They used to give me 100 marks without even checking the paper and then deduct the marks in case they found any mistake. That kind of perfection my each paper had. My mentors had so much of faith on me that they used to ask me not to attend the class, spend some quality time and they would give me the attendance. I made sure that my teachers will have to hunt for mistakes in my paper. I studied each and every concept in depth and my professors never felt like deducting my marks because, my hard work and my dedication were reflected clearly through my paper! I always tried to know what no one knows and going out of my way when it came to studies. Each word spoken by my professors was like a jewel to me! The lessons given by them became my doorway to success and my books became my true companions.

8

Those 15 Marks

The best way to blend my passion for teaching and interest in Management that I could find was to become a Management trainer. I gave a new dimension to my career by pursuing MBA and then preparing the students for MBA entrance examinations.

In the year April 2012, I went to Guwahati to teach the students who were preparing for the CA CPT examination. In my first class, I make sure that I capture the interest of all the students and they listen carefully to everything I say. There was one student sitting on the last bench of the class and dozing off. I was not only angry but curious to know more about that student. After the class was over, I asked one of my colleagues about him. There answers took me by a surprise. They replied that he was one of the brightest students of the class.

My class used to begin at 7 AM in the morning and at 9; I used to give break to the students. One day, I asked that student to meet me after the class. He was nervous and thought that I would scold him for sleeping in the class. After the class was over, he came up to me and asked, "*Yes Sir, you called me?*"

I asked him out of 200 marks, how much marks do you need to top the examination? He fumbled a little and replied "*Sir, 180, or may be 185 marks*". My answer to his statement changed his approach in the class permanently. I said, "*What about the rest 15 marks?*" He was quiet with his head down. I told him "*Don't sleep in the class if you want to score 200 marks and not just 180 or 185*". I promised him that I will help him getting those most difficult and challenging 15 marks.

After this meeting, he made sure that he never missed even a single class and paid proper attention to each and every thing that I explained. He told me, "*Sir, you are meant for teaching the crème of the country and not the masses*". I smiled and thought to myself that the real challenge is to '**find an extra ordinary in every ordinary student**'

He finally scored great marks and got admission in a reputed college. Two months later, I went to Pune for some assignment. He called me saying, "*Sir, your efforts and blessings have shown results and I have finally accomplished my goal of getting admission in a good college.*" He asked me "*Where are you these days?*" I told him that I was in Pune and he was filled with joy because even he was in the same city. He requested me to give a seminar to the students. In my journey of 12 years as a management trainer, I have visited several business schools for giving seminars in order to motivate and guide MBA aspirants, so we finalized a date in July for the seminar.

I asked him to meet me outside the college, and we had a nice conversation for a few minutes before the seminar started. He told me that he got 96% because of which he was successful in getting an admission in that college. I replied that during my time back in 90's percentage never mattered. Only thing which counted was knowledge and eagerness to learn.

9

I am Here

As I entered the auditorium to give the lecture, I could see fresh faces with all the students sitting there scoring above 95%. They felt privileged to be a part of the most respected commerce school of the country. They were cluttering among themselves and I could hear a lot of noise until I started my speech with a very powerful statement ***"You are 96 and you are there, I am 69 and I am here standing in front of you"*** in a loud confident voice!

There was a 2 minutes complete silence in the entire auditorium and every one's attention was completely towards me. That silence made me feel that I have actually accomplished something in my life!

I continued my speech by saying *"**Aham Brahmasmi**"*, a Sanskrit Sootra written in Hindi Upanishads which means ***"I am divine! I am the supreme power and decider of my life! No one has the power to change my decision! I am the owner of my life!"*** I slammed my hand on the podium.

All I can tell you is the secret of your success lies in two simple words **'Determination'** and 'Approach'! If you have these two things in place, you can be rest assured that you will be able to make all your dreams come true. I always had a belief on myself that there is no problem which cannot be solved, and nothing in the world is unachievable.

I am sure a question would have stroked in everyone's mind after hearing my speech that, **what extra efforts I would have put in to reach this level in my life?** My answer to their question is that my exposure to the world of management and experience of teaching Management students gives me an upper edge over others even if I score 69% and they score 96%. No book can provide them the lessons which I gained from my own personal experiences in the field of Management. These lessons have left such a strong impression on my mind that I won't forget them till the last breath of my life.

The secrets which I discovered when I came across different people and different situations are my most prized possessions. I can proudly say **"69 and I am here"** because I have something which cannot be found in the books. I absolutely give credit to my **Willpower** and **Determination** for what I am today.

10

Have a Life, Perform Well

As a Management trainer, I dream to see the same passion, same curiosity in the eyes of my students. The day I am successful in developing same interest and curiosity in my students, would be the day I would feel that I have actually accomplished something in my life.

I want to convey a message to all the students to get above the fear of competition. The more the students enjoy learning without thinking about the outcome of their efforts, the more fortune will smile on them and they will get what they actually deserve.

I can completely understand how much dedication and effort it takes to clear entrance examination for MBA with good scores. Some students sacrifice all the temptations like entertainment, friends and their sleep to achieve high ranks and admission in good business schools. Only the students who are completely focused towards their goal and put constant effort without getting distracted are able to make it to the most wanted business schools.

Who doesn't want to get admission in the prestigious business schools of the country? I guess everyone who wants to pursue MBA, dreams of studying in an MBA college which could prepare them for a brighter future. Now my question is—**How many of those students make real efforts to make their dreams come true?**

Are they not capable of scoring high ranks?

Is there any difference between the students who top the charts and those who are struggling to get admission in a good business schools?

Well, the students who have amazed everyone with their performance are ordinary just like everyone. The only thing which makes the difference lies in their 'Will Power'.

In the beginning, everyone tries to stay focused but once they start facing hurdles in their way of success, they stop right there and are left behind in this race of success. Some of the major distractions include peer pressure and relatives. Students feel that if they avoid hanging out with their friends or conserving themselves from meeting relatives, they might feel left out from the society. Because of this fear, they forget that everything needs to be done within a limit. Locking yourself in a room and cramming throughout the day will not help. No one asks you to cut down your social life. All you need to do is to be wise enough to be able to balance everything.

You need to learn the art of time management which will help you to grasp maximum, in minimum amount of time. Having a personal life is very important for performing well in your studies because it makes you happy and; you can always learn at a faster rate when you are content with your overall life. Cutting down social life will make you dull and negative thoughts would creep into your mind. However, one needs to decide their priorities and know what is more important in different situations.

For example; if you have your exam tomorrow and you have to attend one of your closest relative's wedding; at that time you need to be strong and choose what is more important for you. If you cannot choose one thing then you should be strong enough to be able to balance it out later. It's only the **'will power'** and the **'inner strength'** which can help you to conquer the world.

Consistency is another factor which helps the students in achieving high ranks when it comes to entrance examinations for MBA. Keep in mind that nothing can be achieved in a single day. Have you ever thought that if you would have studied in the same way you do during your exams throughout the year, what difference would be in your career?

You enjoy yourself throughout the year with all your books placed in a corner with dust lying on them ; you finally open them exactly one month before the exam and then you expect to get admission in the most reputed colleges of the country?

In case the students do not get good marks, they have a wonderful excuse to defend themselves, *"The teacher doesn't know how to teach. I wasn't comfortable with his way of teaching."* It is very easy for them to put all the blame on a teacher who has been trying since one year to educate them, taking pains to help them to improve so that you have a better future.

No one can dare to point out a teacher if he doesn't pay special attention to each and every student because he can always say that he can't force a student to study if he is not interested.

One can improve somebody only if the other wants to. Problem with the weaknesses can be handled but changing someone's approach and attitude is not in a teacher's hand. Only **YOU** are responsible for your marks. The teacher will take interest to make you better only if he or she feels that **YOU** are worth it.

If your professors are making efforts to bring you up in spite of your attitude then you must be grateful to them instead of putting your failure on their shoulders.

On the other hand, if you score well, the only credit goes to you and yourself. Why this difference in attitude? I raise this question to every student who considers the faculty responsible for their low scores.

I am not saying that you do not have problems. I absolutely agree that you actually want to study but are caught in the chains of problems like peer pressure and inferiority complex but my dear students; this is what your real challenge is!

No one will sympathise with you for your failure! Your parents might feel bad about it and try to motivate you but all others will be glad about the bitter fact that they scored more than you! You need to gulp this glass of bitter truth and realise that you cannot live your life blaming others!

You need to get over them and believe, that you will be standing in front of several students guiding them the way I do; with the same confidence and sense of accomplishment.

I agree that having a belief in yourself is the first step to success but I would also say that your achievement totally depends on your capability to absorb things.

You can juice up your life with accomplishments *if and only if you expand your container size*.

ROUND 3

What's your Container Size?

11

I cannot play cricket!
I cannot sing!

After coming back from school, I used to take a small nap, quickly finish my homework and spare some time to watch television in the evening before going off to sleep. My only reason for watching television was a hope to listen to melodies sung by my favourite singer; Kumar Sanu. His voice is a perfect example of velvet. It is like a gentle brook flowing over the surface of my heart. Listening to his songs; I started admiring him and wished that even if I could sing half as good as he does, I would consider myself to be a great singer.

Cricket always fascinated me. Watching Sachin Tendulkar batting was a treat for my eyes and my heart raced every time he delivered a boundary or a six. 'Reaching somewhere close to him was one of my most beautiful unattainable dreams'.

The list of my incomplete and unfulfilled desires is endless. In spite of my will and determination; I neither became another Kumar Sanu nor Sachin Tendulkar. I am still Mohit Jain who wears his spectacles and teaches different concepts on a whiteboard to his dear pupils every day.

If we can achieve everything that we really want then why am I still such a bad singer and a poor cricketer?

The answer is simple. We cannot be the best at everything. I fail to do 99% of the things with perfection, but no one can beat me at what I am best and that is **the numbers**.

Not that I did not attempt to improvise my skills as a singer or a cricketer. I joined the cricket camp in order to get more exposure in the field of cricket. I was always made to stand near the keeper because everyone was aware of my amazing fielding skills (sarcasm). 'Slip fielder of the team' was the title awarded to me by my team members. One day, the ball slipped into my hands luckily which became a catch out for the opponent team. I was declared the man of the match that day. To add to it, suddenly everyone wanted me to be a part of their team after that incident; but the fact that '**I cannot play cricket**' remains the same.

I wanted to sing like Kumar Sanu. This desire inspired me to join singing classes. Even after taking my best foot forward; I sounded like a toad. Sooner I realized that I was nowhere close to my favourite singer. My singing was meant only for bathroom and why not; I absolutely enjoyed it; although my family members had to stay at home at their own risk if only they had patience to listen to my melodious voice. No matter how much I try to sing well, the fact remains unchanged, **I cannot sing. Was it because of my lack of dedication and willpower?**

No. I came to a conclusion that **I may not be the best at everything I do but I can definitely do what I am best at.**

How would the world be if we expected Lata Mangeshkar to play cricket and Sachin Tendulkar to sing? Even the thought of it sounds wild. Had not they realized what their true potential was; would they have been as successful as they are now?

Similarly I analyzed myself and came to a conclusion that my real competence lies in numbers. This made me choose the path of numbers and here I am; helping young minds to win over the world of these magical numbers. A world full of wonder, mystery and excitement! That is how I perceive mathematics to be because I love it.

Leonard Euler: Introduced the concept of function, Pi, Euler constant, sigma, iota and trigonometric functions.

Pythagoras of Samos: Discovered the great Pythagoras theorem.

Aryabhatta: Founder of number zero.

Carl Friedrich Gauss: Contributed in notable areas of Mathematics like number theory. Proved fundamental theorem of Algebra and discovered the Gaussian gravitational constant in physics.

These are some of the real life achievers who have achieved a lot in the field of Mathematics because of their undying passion for it.

Not only Mathematics, one can create history in any field they are totally passionate about. For example, Michael Jordan popularly known as MJ, the greatest basketball players of all times came from a completely non athletic background, his father being a mechanic and mother a bank teller. No one in his family had a height of more than 6 feet and his height is 6 feet 6 inches. Even genetically, he fought against all odds and came into this world. He was goofy and an average player as a basketball player. Not many of his classmates liked him and he thought no girl could ever like him.

And look . . . The goofy kid created history in the world of sports with his amazing fighting spirit and competitiveness.

If I would have rather made a consistent effort for cricket or singing; I am sure, today I would have become a cricketer or a singer but I gave priority to one thing which I wanted to do the most.

My extreme passion for teaching and never ending love for mathematics made me land where I am today. I realized that singing or playing cricket is not my cup of tea. I am born to be a teacher and no other job in the world can give me the same pleasure irrespective of the riches, fame or power that they offer.

My dear friends, you do not have to get disappointed if you are not good at everything that you want; because no one can be good at everything. Explore yourself. Figure out which jobs are you made for? Make use of your strength and make sure no one can challenge you at your job. Do not strive to be just good, you have to be the best at whatever you do. Life is easy. We all are different and blessed with one special quality that no one has. The day you identify that special quality, will be the day when your success story will start.

Imagine. Have a vision that you can leave your significant mark on the world, if you believe you can polish your skills to such an extent that no one can beat you. Attain perfection. Whenever you study, never limit yourselves to the books; instead find out other sources to get more information about the topic.

Dream. Desire. Do.

12

If you know how to do something,
it doesn't mean that you should be doing it!

There are many things in our lives that we must know in order to survive. In all these years, I have been travelling for certain assignments and I have made myself efficient enough to do many a things which were not required but helped in my survival. For example; I can do all household work and cook scrumptious dishes by myself. I do not need to order food from elsewhere and spend money unnecessarily every day.

I have learnt driving which is very important to commute from one place to another in Metropolitan cities which have very busy traffic. My car helps me to fight this traffic and reach on time every day.

You all must be familiar with my love for Mathematics by now. I always wanted to teach Mathematics but today there are so many mathematics professors that in order to cement my presence in this industry it became important for me to master other subjects also. I agree that teaching is a noble profession but we all work to earn our livings. Not that I do not want to bring a positive change in the lives of the students by giving good education to them; but charity always begins at home. At that time my circumstances were telling me that I could survive in this industry if I had the capability of teaching subjects other than mathematics as well.

I chose Economics and made sure that I had the knowledge of all the Economics books available in the market, on my fingertips in order to save my students from compromising on the quality of teaching. I gave my more than 100 percent to be the best economics professor in the country because being just good was never enough for me.

Being good is never good enough. If you are doing something then you should be better than the best at it.

Thanks to my undying self belief; today I have introduced several economics books in the market which students read every year and they rely on them for getting good scores in the examination. It feels great!

One day a student came to me and asked "Sir, You have done MBA in finance, why don't you teach Financial Management?

"I am teaching Mathematics and Economics these days and I have never taken Finance classes", I replied.

Surprisingly, the student had more faith in my capability to teach Finance management than I actually had.

I spent one whole month just to polish myself with the Finance management concepts which I studied a couple of years back. I went through all the books available in the market thoroughly, in order to gain perfection in this subject.

Slowly, I mastered various subjects of Management and today I have the ability to teach 13 subjects to the students; each one with equal perfection.

Other professors of the college went up to the higher management and asked "How can Mohit teach all the 13 subjects of Management?" Probably; they might not be aware of the struggle behind being capable of teaching all those 13 subjects; the number of sleepless nights I spent because I never wanted my beloved students to compromise.

A very few people know that I have mastered all the 13 subjects of Management. This is kept as a secret because people think if I say that I can teach 13 subjects then I may not be equally good in all those subjects.

'Is being good at multiple things a wrong thing'?

'Do people start doubting your capabilities if you try to do many things at the same time'?

The answer may be harsh but true; Yes.

This made me realize that though I am good at many subjects, it is not necessary that I should be teaching all of them. Instead; I should choose one path and come out as a winner. Jealousy is an ugly form of admiration. Many of my students forget their own identity and run behind things which they cannot have. If your friend is good at dancing, it certainly doesn't mean that you too have to be good at it and it is absolutely alright if you are not! You do not have to feel that you are any less than your friend. Rather you might be good at something that they would be secretly jealous of.

Most of the people spend more than half of their life being jealous of other's success. If they concentrate on their lives instead of wasting time hating others, they would have been somewhere else in their lives.

Focus on your life. Everything will automatically fall in place. You are digging your own pit by wasting time on envying others.

There are only two kinds of people in this world, one who are jealous and those who make others jealous; it is absolutely up to you what you want to be.

From childhood itself; I respected Shakespeare's writings. *"All the world is a stage"* is a famous phrase from one of his most popular works, 'As You Like It'. We all are performers and have different roles to play on this stage of life. You have to decide what your role is. It is up to you whether you want to be the audience and see others perform; or you want to be a significant part of the play.

Rather than talking about what others are doing or what they should be doing, you should think of what your purpose is in your life; what is stopping you to accomplish your goals and what shall you do to win over your weaknesses. Stop judging others. Get a life. Make your life.

If you know how to do something, it doesn't mean that you should be doing it.

There was a student in my Management class whom I respected for her sincerity towards studies. The only problem that she had was that she always tried to do many things at the same time. She made a complete timetable and divided it in such a manner that she kept some of her time for studies, an hour for going to the gym; some time to prepare for interviews, an hour for learning a new language and a couple of hours to spend time with her closed ones. She was successful in maintaining her timetable for the first few weeks but eventually; she was not able to concentrate even on a single thing and ended up messing up everything.

After a few months, she felt disappointed that she unnecessarily spent so much money trying to do multiple things at the same time. Instead if she would have devoted her valuable time on learning one thing at a time, she would have been the best at least that particular thing.

When the midterm results were announced; she scored much less than her friends who concentrated only on getting good marks in Management classes. She blamed her hectic schedule for her low marks. I asked her, "You blame your hectic schedule for your failure but whom will you blame for making your schedule that way?" In simple words, she herself made her life complicated.

Later, she took a break from everything else and focused only on her MBA classes. She came out with flying colours.

See, you always had it in you. The only thing that went wrong was that you tried to do multiple things at the same time, I told her this congratulating her for her great success on the day of final results.

Two roads diverged in a wood, and I—

I took the one less traveled by,

And that has made all the difference. ~ The Road Not Taken, Robert Frost.

In our life, we come across many situations when we have to choose one path as it is not possible to sail on two boats at the same time . . . .

Which path do you choose at the end?

The one that is easy?

Or

The one that is less travelled?

It needs guts to walk on an unbeaten path but that is what makes all the difference as Robert Frost said in his one of the most appreciable works, The Road Not Taken.

Being an all rounder is remarkable and very few people can actually be good at multiple things. However, my question to you is;

Can you give equal time and concentration on each thing that is important to you?

If yes, I would say, "Go Ahead". But if your answer is 'No' then my advice to you is, it is better not to indulge in multiple things simultaneously. Just like all fingers of the hand are not the same, similarly, not everyone knows the art of balancing all the things beautifully at the same time. You are blessed if you have the power to balance. If you do not, then there is no need to be discouraged. You can be successful in your own way. Choose one thing. Give it your best shot. Master it and then move to the second one. This way you will never have to taste the failure in your life.

Everything that I learnt and did in my life was because of my necessity, circumstances, constraints or even because I was made to do them. Eventually, these things turned from a compulsion to a desire, a desire to learn. I never knew how to cook but the chilly winds of Delhi transformed me into a chef. I was even scared to drive a cycle but the rising fare of auto rickshaw taught me how to ride a bike. I somehow used to pass Economics paper by God's grace but the desire to become a known Economics professor made me master the subject of Economics. No matter what might be the purpose of learning all these things, one thing that I always kept in mind was that whatever I do in my life; I would do it with dedication, honesty and perfection.

I do not expect my students to do everything that they know; I expect them to be the best at everything they do.

13

Searching for a Black Cat in a Dark Room!
There is no cat at all!

Curiosity! It is an amazing emotion which has the power to change the direction of one's life. Being curious is always good but before that one should know what is it all about? If you ask me:

Why the fan runs clockwise and not anti clockwise? Is that curiosity?

If you ask.

Why my name is Mohit and not something else? Is that curiosity?

What I feel is that you cannot call just the urge to find out the answers to everything and anything that you see; curiosity. Instead, if you try to figure out how the motor of the fan runs, that would reflect your eagerness to learn the functionality of the fan.

I can give you an answer to the question: What is the meaning of your name? But not . . .

Why your name is Mohit?

I cannot tell you why the sun rises in the East?

Why birds sing in the morning?

Why rivers flow?

If the man is a descendent of the Apes, why do Apes still exist?

Why pizza boy reaches faster as compared to an Ambulance?

I have seen first year students coming up to me and asking final year questions when they are not even aware of the basic level concepts of the subject.

I never had a problem in explaining to them the high level questions but my question here is that are they prepared to understand them? They need to analyze how much can they absorb, and know what their container size is. You are risking yourself from falling by trying to jump to the topmost step of the ladder without climbing the first one.

I always encourage my students to ask as many questions as possible, no matter how silly their doubts might be. They do not need to be ashamed if they are unable to understand even the simplest concepts. Trust me, it is absolutely alright.

If you are asking today, you won't have to suffer tomorrow.

If you try to pour water in a glass which is already full; you will end up spilling the water. Similarly, you should know whether you are ready to learn the advanced concepts or not. There is no point in jumping to a higher level if you are not even well versed with the 'abcd' of the subject.

You talk about the most prestigious multinational companies when it comes to the question of jobs, but have you ever thought whether or not you are putting in an effort to get placed there; or do you even deserve a job there?

You should be backed up with your hard work and knowledge when you say that you will be placed in the best multinational company.

You must have listened to a very popular phrase, **Curiosity kills the cat** which was used by British play writer Ben Jonson in his 1598 play known as Every Man in his Humour.

If curiosity kills the cat; then we should first try to find the cat, grab her and then kill her. Sadly, my cat is lost in the dark room. She has disappeared in the darkness of unawareness and ignorance. On top of it; my cat is **Black** because anything which is unknown to us can never be bright or colourful; the only colour which comes to my mind thinking of it is **Black**.

Slowly and timidly, I move towards the shadowy, gloomy room which haunts me. At the same time I feel that it beckons me. I can hear the noise of my closed ones, they are shouting and asking me to stop right there. These people include my parents and teachers. They are shouting and want to tell me that I wouldn't find my Black cat in the dark haunted cave. A room full of mystery and desire. In spite of endless attempts of my near and dear ones to save me from going inside, the only thing which I can imagine is the wild green sparkling eyes of my black cat which is calling me. Her call is more audible to my ears than the cries of my loved ones.

Ignoring everyone else, I enter the murky room with the hope of finding my Black cat. I spent the whole night searching for it here and there, I moved in different directions and looked for her in every corner of the room but all I was left with was only the disappointment in the end because there was no cat in the room at all.

Yes, I was trying to find something which did not even exist. I spent the whole night struggling to find the Black cat in the blackish room which was not even there. In the end, I came back with regret, sadness and failure. I asked myself, "What was I doing when everyone was clearly telling me that I was heading towards a wrong direction?" My closed ones were shouting and saying this to me over and over again that I was digging my own pit and I would fall but I never listened to them until I actually got myself hurt.

Even if I decided to go inside the room, did I follow the right approach to find the cat? Had I listened to the people who were trying to illuminate me with the light of knowledge; I would not have been lost in the darkness. If I had a torch with me, it would have been much easier for me to find her.

Right approach, is very important, no matter what you do in your life. I am not saying that being curious is a wrong thing. In fact it is only because of this curiosity that we have been successful in bringing innovations in this world. Had not the great scientist Newton been curious, would he have discovered Gravity just by observing an apple falling on his head? Curiosity can actually do wonders.

I would classify the term 'Curiosity' in two broad terms **curiosity to find out more information or know about something which already exists** and **curiosity to invent something which does not yet exist, but surely can, in the future.**

You can find things that exist through the internet, books, newspapers, magazines, television or external sources or experiences of your mentors and elders. For example; one of your successful friends tells you that he was highly influenced by one of the poems written in a book by his favourite author. The poem changed his life forever. Now, if you are curious to read that poem, what questions would come to your mind? Let me guess.

What is the name of the book and who is the author?

In which Library or book store can I find this book?

Once you find the book, the next question that would click in your mind would be: **On which page will you find the poem which influenced your friend so strongly that his life took a different turn in a positive way?**

In this whole process, if you search for the book in a library where it is not kept, you will not get anything but disappointment. It is very important to look for the right thing at the right place if you want to achieve your goals. Many a times in our lives, we make endless efforts and still fail to achieve what we want. The reason behind this is that we are heading towards a wrong path which will lead us nowhere. Simply making efforts is not enough, it is important to make efforts in the right direction.

For example; you have an exam tomorrow. You do not even check the topics covered in your syllabus. Instead, you read the entire fat book. But when you see the question paper, you find out that in spite of studying so hard, you cannot answer even a single question properly. Saying that you did not work hard for getting good scores in the examination would be wrong. The efforts made by you remained fruitless because of the wrong approach.

Your approach towards things should vary as per the situation. You can make new inventions if you have a curious mind. If you go back several years, there was nothing like air conditioner, LCD television, Smart phone or palm top. The only thing that existed was imagination and vision to bring these things into to a reality.

The desire to discover things which are latent and unexplored is called curiosity. In order to invent them you should first find out answers to the questions like:

What are you trying to achieve?

Is it worth your effort?

How can you achieve it?

You need to draw a thin line between curiosity and stubbornness. Finding out what is hidden is curiosity and finding out something which is non-existent would be nothing but simply stubbornness.

If you try to figure out something which does not exist, without listening to the people who want to save you from falling; you will end up being lost in the darkness. Darkness of incomprehension and in oblivion.

Being adamant is good if it is about achieving your dreams. But showing bullheadedness just to prove yourself right or rather others wrong is foolishness. No one is restricting you from following the call of your heart. It is great that you do what you feel is appropriate but you should at least listen to what others are saying. Might be, they are trying to save you from a major failure because they can see things from a clearer perspective. By 'others', I do not mean to say that you should get influenced or manipulated by the wrong people. My concern here is to explain that if you are blindfolded headstrong and rebellious, you are simply heading towards your own failure. You should listen to everyone but finally do what 'you' feel is correct.

By being closed and unwelcoming to other's advices, you might end up failing in accomplishing your dreams.

Fighting for their rights is the best part about today's youth but it is very important to show rebellious attitude only where required. At the end of the day, we should not lose our humbleness and innocence. I feel that we must listen to people who are elder to us. The reason being, they have seen more life than you, and they have already crossed the stage which you are going through. If you listen to them you might save yourself from a major fall in your personal as well as professional life.

People learn by two ways; either by their own mistakes or by taking lessons from the mistakes that others have committed.

Though it is very difficult to be strong enough to learn from other's mistakes but once you do that, you will be a much happier person.

You can turn your black cat into white with the power of knowledge. Let the light of wisdom illuminate your life and help you to find your cat, 'a white one in the dark room'.

14

Measure your Container's Size

Guwahati, the city of eastern light has given me some of the most important lessons of life. It was a roller coaster ride which showed me different colours of life. I tasted appreciation as well as rejection. This experience was like a dark chocolate which is sweet and bitter at the same time.

In April, 2012, I went there for preparing students for the CA CPT Entrance Examination.

I have been loved and been hated for the same thing which is my blunt nature. I will rather die on my principles, being hated by everyone than being diplomatic.

My students were not just my students; they were my responsibility and I felt that if I could change the track of their lives in a positive way by giving a bitter dosage; no matter how much they dislike me but in the end; I would feel gratified that I was able to do something for them.

After exhausting myself the entire day, I never realized when it was 7 AM and then 7 PM again. Music no more sounded melodious to my ears. It was just another sound. In an attempt of speaking clear so that everyone in the class could understand what I said; I used to speak louder and my vocal chords used to hurt by the end of the day. I loved that pain because I knew that it would pay off at some point.

I cannot be polite and sweet to them always. If I feel that they are lacking somewhere, I cannot shut my mouth thinking that I am getting my salary and their failure would not harm me in any way. I will be rude to them; shout at them; irrespective of the fact of what they think about me.

I used to clearly tell them: **You cannot clear CA CPT Exam if you consider it a joke. If you do not want to study then there is no need to waste your parents' hard earned money.**

Maybe my statements pinched them but weren't they true? Rather than a failure in the end, isn't it better to get a reality check done in advance. Some students might give their best just to prove me wrong; trust me; that day I will be a winner even after losing.

It all depends on their perception. They could either look at my harsh attitude or my real intentions of developing their competencies. It is absolutely their call.

I taught them for hours standing in the class so that they knew the concepts but they took it as a torture.

Did they ever think what would be my benefit of torturing them? Do I enjoy skipping my meals; having sleepless nights and tiring days to give them best teaching? Can't I relax; give one hour lecture and walk away from my class? If you tell me that I am strict so be it; yes that is the way I am and I will not change myself to please anyone, no matter how much you criticize me.

I have seen days when I taught for 11-12 hours and then I heard comments from my own students for whom I was struggling since morning.

'I do not know how to teach'.

'I insult my students or put them down'.

'I taunt my students; in fact I torture them'.

'My students do not want to attend my classes anymore'.

It was very easy for them to find out the flaws in my teaching but practically speaking if I have only a limited amount of time, and I have to cover an entire syllabus which is huge, then I have no other choice but to work at a higher speed. Not that I was running to finish the entire syllabus in a day, in spite of the shortage of time, I spent several hours for each topic and still I got to hear that I was fast?

If you give me a Ferrari which runs at a speed of 100 kilometres per hour then how can you expect me to run it at a speed of a bull cart or a rickshaw? Aren't you asking me to get down; and push the car instead of driving it and still expect me to reach my destination on time without any delay at all?

That day, I apologized to my students and said "I forgot to whom am I teaching. I am just a paid staff member for this institution whose job is to give lectures; complete the syllabus and leave."

It took 9+ hrs to explain classical probability.

5+ hrs and still explaining relative approach . . . .

Same explanation for a class of odd 110 students and still according to you "I am moving fast"

I am unable to understand you.

Fellows, ask yourself first what your container size is.

I walked off the class silently. First time in my life I left my class with my head down and shoulders drooped.

My students wrote an email to the higher management stating that I was explaining too fast and they are unable to cope up with my speed. They also wrote that I insulted them by saying that they should first analyze what their container size is.

That night I sat in disappointment and started writing poetry. My whole life ran like a movie roll in front of my eyes; a movie which had only two colours; black and white. My mistake was that my expectations about life were so high, that I could not reach up to them.

I wrote these lines which perfectly described my situation

"Dhundne chala tha mehngi;

Zindagi sasti ho gayi!

Galti ho gayi"

Some of the students came up to me and said *"Sir, we never had any problem with your teaching. "The other group has it"*. I simply wished them luck and walked out of that place.

Higher management called me and said that these students are very spoilt and habitual of spoon feeding. You will have to explain each and every small thing to them in order to satisfy them with your teaching. I firmly replied, *"I am spending over 9 hours on a topic which can be easily covered in 2 hours explaining every single term and still they are saying that I am fast. If I start explaining them from a very basic level, they will complain that I am underestimating their capabilities by explaining them the concepts which are taught to school students. No matter what approach I follow, there will always be 15 percent students in the class who will not be satisfied with my teaching. I cannot stop my work by getting affected by the comments of those 15 percent students who are blaming me because they are unable to judge their container size. I was not insulting them when I asked them to go and ask themselves what their container size was. I was simply telling them to expand their horizon and realize that they are not in school anymore. They are preparing for a high level entrance examination and they cannot find all the information in the books. If everything needs to be taught from books itself, then what am I here for? They need to compete with millions of students and it is high time that they see beyond those books. I am simply trying to prepare them in such a manner that they can solve any problem from any book given to them. I am going out of my way not to torture them or to make my impression in front of them; I only wanted to give them an extra edge over other students who are preparing for the same examination".*

We have to repeat the same thing at least 100 times for a 3 year old kid in order to make the baby understand. We ask him or her to write the letter 'A' on a piece of paper multiple times every day. Then, we teach each letter to him one by one repeating 100 times a day, 365 days in a year. Similarly, we teach him numbers from 1 to 10. This is because his mind is not matured enough to understand what we are trying to teach him. His brain is like a stone which needs a lot of patience for you to teach every single thing to him. Slowly, this stone develops pores in it and it finally gets converted into a sponge. A Sponge that has the flexibility and capability to absorb everything instantly! Now if I ask you to write English alphabets on a piece of paper, you can do in a matter of few seconds with your eyes closed because your brain has now been converted into a sponge.

It is totally up to the students how they try to understand the concepts in my class. They need to ask themselves, 'Are they ready to absorb what I am going to teach them'. 'Will they listen to me like a sponge or a stone'? If they behave now like a stone, then the only option left for me is to repeat every single word to them hundred times every day which is not possible. I will throw my harsh statements on them in order to correct their approach which is like throwing a stone to them. Now when a stone strikes another stone then it automatically leads to **Fire** and this is what has happened.

All I expect from them is readiness to listen to me and an effort to grasp and understand what I am trying to explain them. It is rightly said that to every action there is an equal and opposite reaction. Even I expect an equal and opposite response for my efforts from my dear students. Without their support, I will not be able to teach them the way I want. In fact, if they are not ready, then no one else either, will be able to teach them. The only thing that other teachers will do is to come in the class, speak for an hour and go without bothering if the students have understood or not. And why shouldn't they? If the students are going to complain to the management for putting extra efforts then isn't it better to simply shut your mouth and leave the class after the lecture finishes.

If they sit in my class as if they do not know anything about the subject and they want to grasp each and every single word that I tell them; then I am sure that by the end of the day they will be able to answer every question from the topic that I taught them. For this, they will have to become a sponge which quickly absorbs whatever is poured on it.

I have always followed a simple principle in my life.

Always prepare for an examination like you know nothing about it; always give an exam like you know everything about it.

This rule has helped me to succeed in life and I am sure that it will help my students grow as well.

15

If You Aim to Fly with Eagles, Stop Swimming with Ducks!

During my stay in Guwahati, I met some students who became very dear to me because I could feel what obstacles they were coming across for being academically competent. I could relate to their situation and realize the reason behind their approach or attitude towards learning and education.

I feel that the job of a mentor is not just to teach students but also guide them to handle the problems or distractions that they face which in turn affect their studies in a negative way.

The CA CPT Entrance Examination includes 4 subjects which are Accountancy, Law, Mathematics and Economics. In order to clear the examination, the students have to score above 100 marks out of 200.

Most of the students have already studied Accountancy in their previous classes which makes it easy for them to have a strong command of this subject.

Law basically includes the theory and a majority of the students find it easy to comprehend. Moreover, this subject is quite interesting to learn and students enjoy studying it.

Mathematics and Economics are the subjects of which most of the students are scared of because these subjects involve a lot of patience and practice. They cannot be prepared one month prior to the examination and students need to give adequate amount of time to them regularly.

If you are not practicing Mathematics or Economics on a daily basis then having each and every topic on finger tips is next to impossible. Not that you cannot go through the entire book in a single go one month prior to the examination but if you wish to achieve mastery in these subjects then you must start studying them from the very first day of the session.

There is no limit to the types of questions that can be asked in a Mathematics or Economics paper. They can be twisted or turned in any way which might confuse the students. Many a times the students know how to solve a problem but they will either get confused or will commit a mistake in calculation; because of which the final answer comes out to be wrong and they end up losing their marks.

Concentration, intelligence and comprehension abilities are some qualities which you should have in order to score good marks in a Mathematics exam. Your marks partially depend on the way you prepare for it and partially on the way you attempt it. You have to ensure that you do not make silly mistakes while attempting the paper.

My question to my students is

Why do you fail to realize that Mathematics and Economics are the most interesting subjects if you start enjoying them?

Although they need consistent practice, they are the easiest, once you understand the concept thoroughly.

Most of the students have the mentality that they are already good at Accountancy and Law and they have to get above 100 marks to clear the examination so they will ignore Mathematics and Economics and focus only on Law and Accounts.

I would say that it is absolutely wrong of them to think this way.

Easy and short path is always attractive but you can reach your destination only if you chose the toughest one.

Similarly, it is very easy for you to study only the subjects which you already know and ignore the rest but will you be able to score good marks by doing so?

Why do you want to live your entire life being an average student? I hear students saying to each other "I do not want anything more. I simply want to clear the examination".

Why is your goal limited only to pass the examination?

You need to think big. If you are weak in a particular subject then you should prepare it so nicely that even your weakness becomes your strength.

If you are already good at Accountancy and Law then you can surely get good marks in those subjects by giving time to them.

However, you need to rather focus on the subjects which you find difficult, so that you cannot only clear the examination but also score well.

One of my students made the same blunder. He simply ignored Mathematics and Economics because he was not good at these subjects. He prepared only for Law and Accountancy and finally his score was less than 100.

He came up to me after the results were declared and said, "Sir, I failed in the examination because of Mathematics and Economics".

"This is where you go wrong. You did not fail because of Mathematics and Economics. In fact, you should give credit to these subjects for these 99 scores that you have got in the examination" I replied in a firm voice.

He asked, "How sir?"

"You ignored Mathematics and Economics thinking that you were good at Accountancy and Law and could easily score above 100. But your good was not good enough. Your favourite subjects could not fetch you marks above 100. I am sure that you would not have scored even this much if Mathematics and Economics were not included in the paper. These subjects got you a few marks even though you did not prepare them. If you would have given equal attention to all the subjects, you would have certainly scored above 100", I responded.

He held his head down after listening to my statement and promised not to make such a mistake in the future.

It is always good to make use of your strengths but it is your responsibility to take care that you do not ignore your weaknesses. *If you are able to conquer your weaknesses then automatically everything else will also fall in place.*

We hesitate to come out of our comfort zones and are inclined towards our old practices. We always want to follow our old ways of doing things and still wish to be called technologically advanced.

Change is inevitable. Change is necessary. If you wish to see yourself at the top of the managerial ladder, you need to follow the pace of time. Everyone loves being updated and purchase the latest products and services. Advanced and latest technologies are most desirable no matter how efficient the old practices were. For example; Windows 8 is the latest craze in the market because of its cool user interface. Older versions are simpler to navigate and have more or less the same functionalities as Windows 8 but new technologies always bring excitement among the audience. They want to try them out. Also, they want to flaunt they possess the latest gadgets which have become more of a status symbol these days. Another example; touch screen phones could be extremely difficult to handle and annoying at times but it was a totally new concept when it was launched in the market. People were delighted to try out something like this.

This is the 21st Century. A fast moving world. One needs to quit old practices and get in sync with time to continue being a part of this race or else they might be left behind.

We all aim high but what do we really do to achieve those heights?

Our dream is to take a flight with eagles in the mighty sky but what does it actually happen in reality?

In reality we tend to move at a slow pace just like ducks swim in the pond.

Right approach could get you right results.

After Guwahati episode, I was engrossed in thinking how to compensate for the time, resources and revenue that had been lost. I decided to thank all the people I came across in Guwahati because somewhere they were responsible for making me find new ways to explore myself.

As our journey reaches towards the end, there are two things that bother us most. Old memories which keep haunting you bringing tears and a smile on your face and the driving force that made you start your journey. Had it been that this force was gone or it was overshadowed by some other artificial forces, you would not have reached so far.

An experience could bring joy as well as melancholy, but one thing that we gain from any experience is learning.

And the Guwahati experience taught me—

If you aim to fly with Eagles, Stop swimming with Ducks.

16

Do Not Ask WHY, Rather Ask HOW!

I always tell my students—Ask me 'How' infinite times and I will tell you but never ask me why. My fight with 'Why' 12 years ago started and it is still continuing. In my mathematics class, whenever I explain a new theorem or formula, there are at least 15 to 20 percent of the students who will always ask me—

Why is this formula used for solving this problem?

Every time I derive the entire formula on the board, knowing inside that only a few students are actually listening to what I was trying to explain. After I finish explaining the derivation; I ask them if they understood it and I will receive a response that they never made an attempt to listen to what I was explaining. I tell them that they need to ask questions like 'why' only if they are ready to understand the depth or the complex logic behind it. I can tell you how things are done but seldom answer that why they are done.

It is rightly said, *If your Boss asks you to Jump, then do not ask why, just ask how high.*

I do not mean to say that you should simply nod your head to whatever higher management says; even if they are being unfair, just to make your position in the organization.

You need to think of this statement from a positive perspective. If someone has seen more life than you then he would have surely already encountered the situations which you are going through right now. They have gone through the same phase and they might have committed the same mistakes which you are going to make. So they know what the right thing to do is and if you trust what they say, you will surely make lesser mistakes.

Even if you feel that you are right and they are wrong, you should still respect their instructions thinking that you have just come out of your shell. May be what they are telling you is actually correct. Be humble to your mentors, parents and elders. A person who gives respect to the opinions of his or her elders always succeeds in life. On the contrary, no matter how intellectual you might be, how much you work hard, if you do not give respect to your mentors and parents, you will never get satisfaction in life. I absolutely agree that there is a huge difference in the mindset of today's youth and the previous generation but you should be flexible enough to bridge this gap between you and your elders.

No one is stopping you to ask 'How'. Your mentors will be more than eager to provide you with the pearls of wisdom that they accomplished in their lives but never question their capabilities by asking them 'Why'.

It is not that only your parents and mentors can teach you the ways of life. Even you have the full right to keep them updated with the things they are not aware of; but you should always maintain your humbleness towards them while you do that.

Make sure that you are not putting them down, taunting them or making them feel inferior to you by bragging about how technologically advanced you are and how old fashioned are they.

I would not blame the students only for the entire situation. I expect flexibility in learning and mutual understanding from both ends in order to fill this gap.

Questions beginning with 'How' can do wonders in your life.

How should I get first position in my class?

How do I make my relationships stronger?

How to get a job in a big company?

If you start finding answers to these questions, your life would become much simpler.

While I am preparing the students for multiple choice questions, I always begin explaining them from the wrong answer. I will pick up the first wrong answer and explain 'why' is it incorrect. Then I will similarly move to other wrong options and give my students reasons 'why' those answers are not right. By explaining my students all the wrong answers I want to tell them 'how' they should not think while answering such questions. I will then finally move to the correct option and the students will already have a reason 'why' it is correct even before I tell them.

You must have heard of the phrase:

Never Argue with Fools. People Might not know the Difference.

If you simply argue without any specific logic, it will only reflect your bullheadedness. A statement supported with proper reasoning and logic is always influential and powerful.

You are free to express what you feel, but again, you should follow a correct approach. Being defensive is a good quality but you should take care that it should be the right situation and right time. If you are arguing simply to put others down, then your personality will be reflected as stubborn and inflexible.

Being curious is good as it allows you to explore life and discover new things. But, you should also follow ethics before putting across a question.

It is not about what is asked; it is about the way it is asked.

Your question might begin with **why** or **how** but if you have the arrogance in your tone, then whatever explanation is being given to you, goes in vain. As a student, you should behave like one. Give respect and keep learning.

Respect is the only parameter which will help you in growing. Learn to give respect and you will earn respect the same way and help yourself to increase your container's size.

So, what's your container size?

ROUND 4

I am a Joker

I am a Joker, The powerful hard
Don't take me for granted, Coz its 53rd card
I have my powers, I can change slot
Till I bow down, And offer what I got
I am a Magical Joker
—M. J.

17

Need to say "No"

Rains have a soothing effect but not when you are in a hurry to reach home after completing daily tasks like giving lectures, marking test papers and preparing for the next lectures. As I was walking out of college, it started raining and I ran quickly to catch an auto rickshaw, across the road. In brevity, I found myself drenched and my shoes covered with mud.

Waiting for the auto rickshaw, I was admiring the beautiful orange sky, looking at the people around, some carrying umbrella and some driving their vehicles. I was flabbergasted to see a man who was enjoying tea at the tea stall across the road. I could not believe my eyes that it was Ravi, my classmate. The quiet boy of our school with big spectacles who would always be engrossed in his own world of books and never score less than 92 percent. With his consistent efforts, dedication and focus, he became an example for rest of the students. In the contrary to my expectations, he was wearing slippers and simple clothes. I greeted him with a hug and asked him,

"How are you? What are you doing these days?"

He looked at me sorrowfully and said, "I met with an accident a few years back because of which everything went otiose. I was bed ridden for six months and could not complete my studies. After that, getting a job in this rat race was a huge challenge. I had so many responsibilities to fulfil and I took whatever job I could get my hands on. The fire to excel died and eventually I got used to this life."

I instantly replied to him, No! You still have the potential to be successful. If you would have said 'no' to that job and pursued further education or searched for a better job, you would have been victorious today. I informed him about vacancies in my own college and assured him that he can surely make a new start. He smiled and said "I will see."

We both enjoyed that small cup of tea and then I realised that rain had already stopped. I gave him my business card and asked him to be in touch. He never messaged, called or met me again. Even today, amongst random thoughts when I think of him; a question that comes to my mind is: Why did he not say no to the situations and come out as a winner?

I know many of us fail to accomplish our dreams because we could not say no to our parents, friends, teachers, relatives or jobs. Keep faith, wait for the right thing and sooner or later you will get what you deserve.

My childhood friend who has now become a Manger in an IT based company requested me to give a seminar on the latest technologies and software available in the market. Respecting our 15 years of friendship, I humbly said "No" to him because I am a management trainer and my knowledge about software is petite. With my exceptional knowledge of Mathematics, Accountancy, Economics, it is certain that I can guide aspiring Management students to accomplish their goals but that does not mean that I will be proficient in every field.

Increasing your container size and showing interest in learning new things will definitely help in accelerating your career but you need to understand that you cannot be best at everything.

As a student, I always took all the assignments given to me very seriously. My project report was the hottest commodity in the class as my class mates used to copy it and score as good as me. Every time I planned to study, someone or the other relative invited our family for dinner or suddenly my friends would start calling me. It was difficult to say, 'No' to my near and dear ones but the fact was that if I kept saying yes to all of them, I would end up putting my future in trouble.

After a series of failure because of these distractions, I decided, that I need to say "No" firmly if I wished to achieve my targets.

18

Anything which can be inflated doesn't burst.
But it can!

Inquisitiveness encourages exploring the world of opportunities and taking the first step towards the destination. With a curious frame of mind, learning becomes interesting and effortless.

The word "Inquisitiveness" reminds me of Jyoti, my student who asked me a lot of questions during lecture. Her sincerity towards studies was clearly reflected through the kind of attention she paid to every word that I spoke. Her scrutiny and thoughtfulness was commendable, supporting me to explain each theory in depth. She was an active participant in poetry recitation, article writing, singing and dancing competitions organized in college every year. What an outstanding performer she was! Getting consistent appreciation for her talent and hard work made her a content and confident person. Even though she scored well in all the exams but she was unbeatable in English. Sooner she realised that she has a creative bend of mind and she should go for a job profile which would give her a platform to make use of her talent and skills. Today, she is doing P.HD. in English from an internationally renowned university.

I feel that the decision that she took is legitimate and all of us should decide our career on the basis of our skills.

Ask yourself, How far can you go to rise in life?

Who decides how much effort do you need to put in order to accomplish your targets?

Is it your parents who have invested their time, money and energy for your career or is it your teachers who have left no stone unturned to prepare you for your future or is it your friends who have motivated you when you lose hope?

It is no one else but you! No one can decide what you really want in life except you. Others might show you the right path and give you choices to go for but until and unless you work hard towards your goal in an organized manner, no one can help you.

It is very rightly said that God helps those who help themselves. When I passed out from my college, all my friends took a different career path. Some went for further studies, some got married and some started working. A few of them are still doing nothing. Trust me, the trauma of not getting a job after completing graduation can immensely hurt the self-esteem of any person. One of my closest friends was facing turmoil when he was not able to choose a career path for himself after graduation. He was in an oblique state of mind *(neither perpendicular nor parallel)*. Every person used to come up with different suggestions and in the midst of all this he felt discouraged, confused and disappointed. At one corner of his mind, he wanted to go abroad for further education. His parents suggested to him to take Banking PO exams. Some of his friends advised him to start his own business and couple of relatives recommended him to rather leave everything and follow his passion, music as a mainstream career.

Out of all this he decided to do nothing. He used to sit at home, sleep, eat, and watch television and again go back to sleep. He became indifferent to the harsh comments, rebukes and insults of the people around him. Even though being a single child, he did not realise his responsibilities towards his parents. I could feel that he was a victim of self-guilt which was eating him from within but he felt helpless and lacked energy to break free from the chains he was tied into, and work towards his goal.

No counselling worked for him. After a couple of months, he broke down completely and locked himself in a room for a couple of hours. He gave a deep thought to what he was doing with his life and how he could make his way in this competitive world.

Everybody observed a change in his behaviour after that. He took out a pen and a paper and prepared a plan for his next 6 months. The very next day, he purchased Quantitative Aptitude books with his own pocket money and started reading newspapers too. He prepared a powerful resume for himself and started searching for jobs in the banking domain actively. First few months were really difficult for him as he had to travel 2 hours every day to attend interviews. Every time he got rejected, there was no disappointment on his face. In fact, he analysed where he went wrong and worked towards his weaknesses. Not only that, he also joined Verbal Ability classes and woke up every morning at 5 a.m. to attend them. He made it a routine to practice everything which was taught in the class. His positivity, confidence and determination surprised everyone and finally after being a ferret for a couple of weeks, he got a job in a well-known nationalised bank. The success that he got is very well deserved. I must say, "Hats off to his sincerity and desire to achieve his goal."

The same goes for all of us. It is only you who can decide what you want, how can you get it and what all you need to do in order to achieve it.

Most of the time, we try to find out qualities which people around us have but in this process we forget who we actually are. Instead of struggling to do many things at the same time, it is always better to concentrate on one thing first and move to next only after gaining expertise in the former.

It is rightly said, "Excess of everything is bad." Most of us either would not initiate efforts for achieving our targets. And if we do, we are incapable to evaluate where to stop.

It is true that expanding your container size is an outstanding way to actualize your potential but having an unclouded picture of where to draw a line is also crucial for your progress. For example; you are preparing for an Entrance Examination in which equal credits are given to each subject. Now if you have started Mathematics first and you have exam in another 3-4 days then you should know where to stop and start preparing other subjects.

Full stop is the most important character of every language without which everything is ambiguous and meaningless. Similarly, in your personal life, you must know what is appropriate for you and where to halt.

Being best at one thing is more valuable than being just good at multiple things. Figure out what are you good at. When I asked my students "Tell me one thing you are best at?" Some of them answered "Nothing Sir!" At some point, we all feel that we are good for nothing but this only means that we do not know ourselves completely.

One of my maternal cousins is laudable when it comes to playing Cricket. He has won several State level championships and has a very bright career in this field. On the other hand, I could hardly play the game. Just by looking at him, I went through plethora of emotions like happiness, jealousy, desire, admiration, sadness and inferiority complex. In an attempt of playing better than him, I ruined other things as well. Even after several efforts, I failed to make it up to his level. Does that mean that I am good for nothing?

The eagerness to learn Cricket is appreciable but soon I realized that I was messing up other aspects of my life just because I was trying to achieve mastery at everything I do.

The passion, the desire to succeed is good but there is a very thin line between desire and greed.

"There is no fire like passion, there is no shark like hatred, there is no snare like folly, there is no torrent like greed."
—Gautama Buddha

Our 'Ego' never lets us accept defeat and we run blindly after the things at which we fail just to satisfy our ego even if we do not need those things anymore.

I have always seen devotion in my students for clearing MBA entrance examination in order to get admission in reputed business schools. The passion with which they prepare for the exam is commendable. Some of the students would make it big with their consistent efforts and hard work, but spark within them dies once they get what they have been trying for. *The reason is that we, human beings take things and people for granted. We value or desire something only till we bring it to a successful conclusion.*

Even I have gone through the same stage; and message to my students is *"Value whatever you have.* **You need it, you do not want it. And if you want it, you do not need it. There lies difference between desire and demand.**

The day you put your self-pride aside, you will realise that some things are just not meant for you but that does not imply that such things are beyond your reach. The term *'Quit'* might be against your amour-propre but sometimes it is wise to abdicate on something which is not showing expected results despite several efforts; and rather concentrating on other aspects in which you are unconquered and unsurpassable.

At the end of the day it is all about knowing yourself and analysing your skills.

As William Shakespeare said, **"Be not afraid of greatness; some are born great, some achieve greatness, and others have greatness thrust upon them"**

There is nothing in the world which you cannot achieve. All it takes is hard work, dedication, consistency, proper planning and of course execution. You might be naturally good at a particular skill and you can excel in life if you pursue your career path accordingly.

Let us talk about a man who is honoured as the pioneer of the personal computer revolution. He is one person who has become a role model for the people who wish to succeed in IT industry. He is a synonym for inspiration. His biological father Abdulfattah "John" Jandali and biological mother, Swiss-American Catholic Joanne Carole Schieble brought gave birth to a child who created history. As his parents were students at that point of time, their relationship was not accepted by Carole's family. They gave Steve for adoption. He was raised by Paul Jobs and Clara jobs. His father Paul Jobs worked as a carpenter and a mechanic. Though they were not very financially secure, they wanted to give the best education to their special child who lit their world with happiness. Paul taught him rudimentary electronics and how to work with electronic gadgets. This seeded strong interest in him for electronics. He took his first job as a technician at Atari Inc. in late

1973 in Los Gatos, California. His employers believed that he was a computer wizard. A person who had the abilities and knew how to present them. He along with his friend, another computer wizard, Wonznaik invented blue boxes, a device used for making long distance telephone calls. And it all started from there . . . .

Once Steve said that if there were no blue boxes, there would have been no Apple Inc. today! World's second largest information technology company in terms of revenue.

There are many lessons that we can take from his life:

- Everything happens for good.—Hadn't he been adopted by Paul Jobs, he would not have developed a keen interest in electronics. His life, his world might have been entirely different than whatever it is today.
- Make use of your skills—Steve Jobs is Steve Jobs today as he always made use of his potential. He gave wings to his dreams by following his passion which was computers.
- Build a strong team of players—He was able to discover Apple inc. along with his techie friends Steve Woznaik and Ronald Wayne. All three of them were masters in the field of computers and they joined hands, magic happened.
- Believe in yourself—Most importantly, he always believed in himself. Though he had to sleep on the floor in his friend's Dorm. Though situations were not always in his favour, he believed in himself . . . .

There is a successful person like him hidden within each one of us; all we need to do is discover that successful person.

The thought of being good at multiple things gives you a feeling of self-gratification and confidence. However, nothing great can be achieved in a day. Everything takes time. If you wish to excel in different fields, take one thing at a time. Become a master by covering up the entire horizon and then move up vertically to next thing.

It is advisable to stay in a particular job role for a few years in order to gain knowledge, sharpen skills and get familiar with the different approaches of the job before moving to higher level to become luminary. *'The deeper the foundation, the stronger the fortress'.*

Same concepts are taught in Mathematics from high school till post-graduation, what differs is the complexity. One should know alphabets before being able to read or write. Similarly, if basics are strong then rest will fall in place.

That is why; every chapter begins with the simplest concepts and then gradually moves to the difficult ones. *By conquering the horizon i.e. gaining expertise in the field that we are in, our basics will be strong which will in turn help us when we chose another horizon by moving up vertically.*

By having a dynamitic personality, you will be able to gain knowledge and proficiency in every field. However, if you do not scrutinize what interests you and try to feed everything in your brain, then you will end up moving in circles in the search of corners. Have Guts to say "No". Draw a line where you want to stop. Think horizontally before you plan to rush vertically and thus you will be able to eliminate that '*oblique state of mind too*'. Throughout your life, you see, hear and feel different things; it is all up to you what you wish to remember or give importance.

Success always starts with failure.—Tim Harford

19

Stop not till the Goal is reached!

Every time I remember the days back in 1992-1993 when I used to have a long walk to school every morning with my buddy carrying heavy school bag on our delicate shoulders, I get a smile on my face. On our way, we used to discuss how to escape from teachers' scolding in case we had not completed our homework or prepared for the test. We used to kick a stone along a slender gully and then went out of our way to kick it again till we reached school. There was a much simpler and shorter route to the school but we still preferred to choose the mystic, adventurous longer one. The reason being we hoped to see cute girls near the girls' hostel. Every day, we used to set our journey with the optimism of getting attention from at least some girl but all in vain.

We even tried to make interesting hair styles, wore shiny polished shoes, ultra white shirt but still no results.

However, if we would have continued traversing the same path without fail, we would have surely got lucky someday.

We left going through our old long route when exams were near and the only thing we could think of was cane on the bums that we would get from parents as well as teachers in case we fail in exams. We sacrificed our so called love and got back to studies!

I was in 8th standard at that time. We still have a couple of laughs every time we think of those good old days.

"Stop not till the goal is reached" was the motto of our school and these words have the power to alter the path of your life. Many a times, we get tired after several attempts and quit. Had we pushed ourselves a little hard, success would have come as a surprise. Very few people continue the course and after reaching the goal they realise that they had taken the right step of not giving up when they were so close.

Anything done half-heartedly or incompletely cannot give expected results. If you stop making efforts at the last moment, all the hardships that you have taken to achieve your goal will be fruitless. Just when you get tired or disappointed, get up and say to yourself *"Just a few more steps and I will see my dreams come true."*

Nothing in the world is achieved conveniently.

As an infant, were you able to take the first step without falling?

Would an infant be able to utter first few words without fumbling?

Nothing can be achieved in the first go. Perfection can be attained only with practice. If you try to solve a mathematical chapter for the first time, it might take you entire day to finish all the problems. Once you revise the chapter several times, you will be able to finish it within an hour.

This reminds me of one of my brightest students who failed in Mathematics even after being sincere and regular in studies. He never missed a single class and made sure that he practiced every concept that was taught in the class but still he could not score well during the mid-term examination. This was the time when he needed to figure out where he went wrong and how could he improve his performance. Instead, he stopped making efforts at all thinking that he is not good enough. Eventually, his score dropped even more during the final exams. May be if he had not stopped working towards his aim when the situations were difficult he would have shown tremendous improvement in his scores. Our motivation plays a very important role when our body and mind gives up. We never know we might be very near to our destination when we stop moving towards it. Had we walked a little more, we would have reached our destination.

Have you ever tried to solve a query and leave it in between if you are unable to understand the concept? I am sure all of you must have come across such a situation while preparing for exams. Make sure you put in all the efforts to try and understand the concept and in the end; you might realise that it is not so difficult at all.

Unless and until you get what you desire, never stop trying to get that.

20

My Best in Everything!

*"Life is all about how you take it
and not how you make it".*

For me, the Cadbury project was like a roller coaster ride. My maternal uncle who stayed at Agra had close association with the distributors of the company. I still remember the bike ride along with my friend from Delhi to Agra to meet my maternal uncle in order to get complete information about the project from distributors of the company like market of the product, how it works, sales and latest products launched by the company. He was flabbergasted to know that I rode on my bike continuously for hours together that too in such a harsh kind of weather just to meet him. That minor project meant a lot to me and I wanted to make it successful at any cost.

I always try to give my best into everything I wish to learn or accomplish. During my first job, several projects were assigned to me. Our team consisted of 4 members and different responsibilities were assigned equally to each person. Success of a project depends on the attitude and perspective of team members towards it. In every team, there is at least one member who wants to make least efforts and shrugs away his/her commitments thinking that finally the credit will go to the entire team so how will one come to know how much effort has been made by each person. This lethargic person's attitude can prove to be very harmful as even if the overall project is good; if you have not done anything to make it happen then you will not gain any knowledge or experience.

How long can one depend on others for work? May be in future, you are put in some team where no one is ready to help which leaves no choice but to work on own. Now if you say that you do not know how to do things even after working in several projects before, there will be a big question mark on your integrity regarding your work.

Active participation while you are working is definitely good as it not only enables you to do the work in an effective manner but also develops your overall personality. However, it is also important to take care that you are not dominating other team members. Each person should be given equal opportunity to come up with new suggestions, ideas, strategies and plan of action. You might never know what might work wonders for the project. So, opinion of every person should be respected. After collecting all the ideas, each of them should be analysed and scrutinized. Finally, the strategies which are profitable, reliable, risk free and effective should be implemented in order to complete the project in a successful manner. Arrogant and stubborn behaviour affects the overall performance of the team in a negative way as new ideas cannot be discussed and other members might feel discouraged and eventually lose interest in the project. You don't become a leader by being bossy or controlling. Instead, it is your duty to maintain cordial and peaceful work environment in the team.

While working in a team, a few people think only about their own career growth and neglect others and some of them focus only on the success of overall project. People belonging to second category are more successful as rather than their own selfish motives, they are more concerned about making the task assigned to them successful.

For some, a person who is trying to bind the team and making efforts to leave no stone unturned in order to make the best out of all the available resources is a Leader; for others he is nothing but a Joker who is not getting anything in the end after slogging for such a long time.

Similarly, if you want something passionately, then you will automatically find out ways to do it. For example, if a small kid likes chocolates, then no matter wherever you hide them, the kid will definitely find them out when you are not at home. This is the power of desire. The desire which no one can inculcate in you but it comes only from a superfluous urge to do everything that is possible to get your job done. The go getter attitude lights a spark within you that says, you are something, you are special and no one can stop you from winning in every sphere of life.

21

Treat your Neighbour as your Enemy!

Let me share one of my real life experiences. During my college days, my notes and assignments were so popular at the small Xerox shop in our campus that if the shopkeeper would have displayed, "Mohit Jain's notes available here" in and around his premises, he would have made fortune out of it.

After completion of my course, we had to submit dissertation and its acceptance was very crucial for my future. I was quite confident about myself because of the kind of research I had done on the given topic. Thorough study and hard work was clearly reflecting through my dissertation and I spent a lot of time to make it unique, influential, and interesting and of course informative. It was supported by statistics, facts and real life implementation.

Everyone in the class knew that I was a reliable source of knowledge. I never stepped back to help my classmates because according to me, it was the best way to revise my own concepts. Having a thought of not guiding others with a fear that they might perform better than you is nothing but a sign of insecurity and lack of confidence. In fact, group study is one of the best ways to clear doubts and have a stronger hold in different concepts. One can discuss different ideas among friends and then come to a common positive conclusion.

There were some of my classmates who never attended classes and requested me most of the times to give proxy for them. For them, bunking classes was fun and escapism from boring lectures. However, everyone was damn serious about the final year project as it played a crucial role in getting good placement.

My classmates who were not in terms throughout the course also came up to me to seek help during dissertation. Not being academically strong, one person chose to sit only next to me throughout; and over a period of time, he became one of my closest associates. He struggled for several months after completion of secondary education because of less marks. With a lot of difficulties, he got admission to our college and now he wanted to leave all the fun aside and make up for the mistakes that he had done in the past. He did not even miss a single class during the course and we used to study together for hours on weekends. We used to share top places amongst us most of the time. I prepared the entire dissertation for him as I believed that he was my buddy and helping him was my duty. The dissertation that I wrote for him was not only accepted but also highly appreciated. You call it misfortune that my own dissertation was not accepted and I had to rewrite it. Out of distress, I questioned myself, "Is helping your closest buddy a sin and get yourself punished for the same?" We encounter multiple situations in our life when we help others and take a hit as a consequence.

In such a situation, what would you want to do? Vouch for self or others? *In a competition, no one has pals. If you have to win, you have to walk alone.*

22

Mohit Jain
B.Com, MBA, RAT, CAT

Getting a job was not difficult. In fact, some good opportunities were in hand but maybe I had some other plans. I do not know what to call it, a mistake or the best decision of my life.

Truly said, one should never be afraid to experiment in life. Either you will succeed or you will learn some important lessons of life. At the end, you will become a trainer, a true guide for others saving them from committing the same mistakes.

After returning from Delhi, I wondered, "What next?" All I did was take rest at home and chat with friends. My life had become similar to a race between RAT and CAT in which neither RAT loses nor CAT gives up. I was tangled in these situations. My strengths became weaknesses for everyone else. I was in a dilemma.

"Your son has done MBA then why is he still not working?", "Is he planning to do his own business?" Such comments from near and dear pierced my heart. My parents tried explaining to me the humiliation that they faced in the form of suggestions.

I knew where I was going. Leaving my path and bowing to the circumstances was my first defeat. Actually, the decision was not that bad too. When I turn back and look into my past, I feel that I was meant to be where I am.

Someone with the sole purpose of making "win-win" situations for all could not be anything else but a Joker. And now, this Joker is stepping into the market in his real form. My face reflected the games that life was playing with me. I realised that life is all about selling your skills. This was my first step to be a Salesman. Yes, I am a salesman. I am a Joker.

23

Rs. 4,000 it was!

Scrutinizing the employment newspaper with the hope of finding opportunities had become my daily routine. One fine day, particular column on that paper caught my attention. I stood up from my chair, dressed myself up, buffed my shoes shiny, wore a tie and rushed to the venue.

I kept in mind all important tips which would help me to crack the interview. My emotions were taking a roller coaster ride. Citibank being the global brand, my thoughts started running, I visualized the work place, environment, my role and responsibilities in the company. Contrary to my expectations, the office did not look like Citibank from *any-angle*. It was a *backup* office and the job role being offered was Direct Sales Associate which included selling of loans.

Training will be provided after which field work, cold calling would be assigned.

This was my first step towards direct marketing concepts. No matter what work you do, you will always gain something at the end. The practical knowledge and experience will help in some or the other way. In spite of being a finance graduate, I was learning marketing and establishing contacts with different people. For me, watching how others sell their products was the best way to learn marketing skills.

In the end, I learnt that no matter how good the product is, I will not be able to sell it if I cannot sell my own skills. Hence, I became *'salesman of Mohit Jain'*. Within first 23 days of the job, all the targets assigned were achieved. I laughed at myself and watching that, people laughed. I started enjoying the essence of life. At least, I got ready by 8 a.m. in the morning every day and worked till 8 p.m. in the evening. My productivity increased which in turn boosted my self-confidence.

4000 Rupees. Yes, the first pay cheque of 4000 Rupees was indeed the most esteemed asset in the entire world for me. I was learning valuable lessons in my life and started looking for new definition of happiness. I found my identity which made me feel out of the world. I was ready to win and make others winner too.

If I would not have met my friend that day, I would have remained a Joker throughout my life.

24

Cycling from Naxal to Thamel

"This company is in Kathmandu. I gave my interview yesterday. *Even, you should submit your CV*", he told me and the very same day I reached Kathmandu to sell myself but this time in a different atmosphere, different market and among different people. This change taught me new ways of selling myself. *Survival was indeed a challenge for me as soon as I realized that no one would help me grow in life. I have to pave my own way to the doorway of success. No one will ask if I have work in hand or what work I do.*

Your co-workers who say to you "There is no work today, just sit and enjoy", will laugh at you in the same way they laugh at a Joker if you are not in a position to submit your daily work report to your boss. '*Your deeds should be a result of your own thoughts and not that of others'.*

I understood that the journey from Working Men Hostel at Naxal to Company's Headquarters at Thamel is the only time slot that I get to think of what to do, where to go, whom to meet, which presentation to make, how much to sell myself, how much profit to make so that in the evening; I could proudly present my daily report to the boss and get a pat on my back.

I have developed the art of visualising things which do not exist to perfection. I started talking to myself and realized that there are many more qualities of a Joker in me which need to take a tug with the qualities of a salesman. I decided to throw away the conic hat of the Joker and wear a tie of a salesman which was needed indeed.

If I look through my eyes the journey between Naxal and Thamel is just a route between two places for namesake, it was more like a spool of film roll moving in front of my eyes showcasing my entire day's activities.

25

K2K
B2K

As soon as I started enjoying fruits of my efforts, I got a hard blow. "*We cannot help you to grow up the ladder beyond this stage even though we are very impressed by your excellent work. We are bound by our company policies.*"—said my Manager to me, one fine morning. When you get stalled, what would you do? Will you stand still or would you continue in search of new prospects because plague grows only in stagnant water.

The real identity of water is confirmed only when it is flowing. It will hit bedrocks and eventually find a new course while everyone thinks that it has reached standstill.

I took a five day leave from the company to visit Agra for my cousin's wedding. While returning, I had to catch a train from Kolkata to reach Kathmandu. I boarded the train, looked for my berth and settled. Then my Father asked, "Why don't you come back to Kolkata? We have numerous opportunities over here as well!" And my mind started running. I started thinking, "Do I need to start from level zero? But I would be with my parents!" Black and White cat started fighting within—*It hardly matters whether your cat is black or white, till it catches mice.*

First step of my career began in Kathmandu, where I learnt how to wear a tie. I have to do the same job but in different conditions over here at Kolkata. Here I have learnt the basics of direct marketing. My perceptions towards things changed altogether after I started working in Kolkata.

26

Salesman of the Day

"Learning by doing" should be given equal emphasis as academic learning for better understanding and real life implementation of the concepts learned in the classroom. Going beyond textbooks is fundamental to traverse the untouched, unspoiled path of enlightenment and tell the world about magnificence of your journey.

The theoretical learning confined within the four walls of the classroom at various levels of education is mostly forgotten after a certain period of time if it is not combined with testing or execution in the social environment. Cramming might fetch good academic scores but will you be able to achieve true mastery over the subjects?

While being a consultant in Management, my interest in tertiary level of education has developed immensely over a period of 14 years. Through my experience, I have realized that all the learning is confined to four walls of an AC room. The trainees are not well equipped to practice the ideologies which were taught in the confined environment and as a result there exists a shadowy picture of what you have learnt and what you have to implement.

It gives me a sense of déjà vu and takes me back to the days when I was a management trainee in the field of direct marketing. This experience taught me precious lessons in my professional and personal life. Marketing "FUNCITY" discount cards was one of the challenging tasks assigned to us. The only time we reproduced the lessons that we learnt was during dawn and dusk. We used to put our heads together to bring out new ideas for achieving the daily tasks and through which we used to motivate ourselves. This 3 months journey was like an erupting volcano. The room echoed with the incantation of JUICE (Join Us In Creating Excitement) by all enthusiastic fresh minds. The conviction to go out on the field was commendable.

I learnt the prominence of time and discipline. We had to complete the assigned task well within the allocated time. As per the estimation, we had to meet at least 200 people, which mean 25 people per hour within the territorial limit. Time, target, these were the two most pivotal aspects in midst of effective marketing and networking.

I recognized the fact that "The law of averages" is not just illustrative but also factual. As per vision set by our team managers who have achieved mastery in this field affirmed that after every 24 negative responses, there will be one positive response. My marketing experience on field proved the same. I actually made 24 unsuccessful attempts before successfully marketing one fun city card. Therefore the motive of each trainee was to hit this 'Law of Average'.

Sense of achievement is the biggest driving force of Success. However, every accomplishment comes at a price. One can reach pinnacle of glory only after a series of rejections. Facing rejections is a challenge. It either makes you **'bitter'** or **'better'**. It is up to you what you want to become.

Rejections like 'door slams', 'rudeness' and 'ignorance' led to depression and sadness amongst the management trainees which was then converted into anger and passion.

Thanks to our mentors who not only imparted in us skills to become "salesman of the year" but also provided moral support which kept us going irrespective of how difficult the situations were. They taught us the virtue of self-belief.

You can and you will became our mantra. Post 8 hours of grooving on-field learning, the entire training room echoed with the rounds of applause for the trainees who successfully marketed 8 coupons. A ring of bell was given as an honour for their efforts making them forget all the disappointments and dismissals they faced during the day. This stirred other trainees to get the next "Ring of bell" for them.

What's more! Any trainee receiving three bells was designated as a team leader which motivated them further to keep the team strong and united. Sense of accomplishment sowed seeds of aspirations within us preparing us for a better tomorrow.

Dealing with people having different temperaments, ideologies, attitudes and personality is an art. Being a salesman, you need to follow different approaches for selling the same service or product to different people. The customers should always feel that they have made a smart deal at a best price. Presentation skills, confidence, good usages of words are some qualities that a salesman should have; to turn potential customers to real customers.

Direct marketing is much more than door to door target-oriented commodity selling. It involves a vision to be able to bring out fresh ideas and concepts which would generate strong, stable and long term network or relations. It is oriented towards "how and why" rather than what.

I ask to myself;

Who is a salesman? A person who wears a tie and rings your doorbell?

Every day, a new journey began, under the scorching heat, I walked, door to door, with a goal in mind, goal of marketing 8 coupons per day. Different people! Different reactions! Different temperaments! Whenever I rang the doorbell of a customer, or I should rather say, potential customer; my heart raced; I always had an insecurity that the person opening the door might feel that I, *"the salesman"* was invading their space and time. My real achievement was not in the number of coupons I sold; my major concern was to make the customer feel happy about their decision. Being a direct management trainee, I feel that my customers should not feel that they have wasted 'precious 5 minutes' that they gave to me from their hectic schedule. I had to prepare a different strategy to advertise the same product in front of different clients. Figuring out one good reason, they should purchase the coupons was a real challenge; as this reason was different for every customer! And that's what separates direct marketing trainee from a salesman. The fact that I will have to pay from my own pocket in order to make up for the loss in case I am unable to sell even one coupon a day, fuelled my zeal to succeed.

This experience, unquestionably, boosted confidence amongst the trainees. It helped me to overcome the fear of rejection, door slams and rudeness. It taught me how to introduce self to a customer having limited patience and interest. Now, I have the nerve to address everyone with certitude and perfection. Not only has direct marketing upgraded and tested my analytical skills but has also boosted me to become a good orator, embracing clarity of thoughts. On field experience and practical engagements have prepared me to deal with unexpected and unknown circumstances.

The wisdom that I have attained during that 3 months internship period by following a common sense based approach, could never be discovered or unzipped being caught in a vicious circle of cramming concepts and putting them on a piece of paper in an examination hall.

This wonderful milestone seeded desire of teaching within me; I wanted to follow the footsteps of my mentors and provide practical knowledge to my students. I truly wished to communicate the lessons that I had learnt and share my experiences with them. This was the beginning of a new phase in my life.

27

Karmasthali
The Platform to Perform

"Experience is the best teacher"

Being one among the many who truly believes in practical knowledge, I wanted to impart the cream of whatever I had learnt via field experience as a Management trainee and Sales Executive, to aspiring young minds so that they could break free from the chains of bookish knowledge and learn something which they could actually implement in real life as management graduates.

World is a dynamic place where one needs to be aware of acting and reacting dynamically. There are certain things which you would learn only by implementation; which cannot be found printed anywhere; they can be learnt only by experience of one's own and others.

There was a fire ignited inside me during my journey, flaming my wish towards setting up an institution and encourage young people via my experiences.

This gave birth to *"Brain Twister Tentacles"*, an establishment with a vision.

To emerge as a centre of excellence, innovation and learning proactively; catalyzing the growth of education sector through motivating, and leading professional and academic education, with concern for social welfare and human values.

To be a pioneer in delivering education with a definite different touch, we will be thoughtfully bold and set our own standards. We will ensure that each of our students becomes an enthusiast by anticipating their individual needs, potential and requirements and by providing top notch services that reflect the imaginative fusion of the best processes and the best one can get.

More is yet to come . . . . Platform is endless . . . . Aims are high.

Started off with a fistful of students within four walls of an economical room; teaching Mathematics and Economics; the "Joker" flourished real fast, as my students liked the teaching methodologies and they started comparing it with other.

Slowly, the Brain Twister Tentacles emerged as a promising institute and transformed itself into Karmasthali Institute of Management Studies.

The name Karmasthali derived from a Sanskrit word has been very carefully chosen as it signifies exactly what each endeavoring soul aspires, "A platform to perform".

*"**Karma**" has a lot of influence in our lives. Do we get what we deserve . . . . or do we deserve what we get? If we take care of our karma, the karma takes care of everything else. Magic happens when action meets opportunity. Be prepared, no one knows when will an opportunity knock the door. One moment of success will overpower years of struggle done behind it. All we need to do is to look for that 'one moment' that could change our lives.*

Being an apostle of Karma, I felt that no name other than 'Karmasthali' could chime with this organization. Proving self at every stage is the greatest challenge but a fact of life. By the time one achieves perfection in a particular domain, he/she realizes that the concepts that he has mastered are already obsolete. There is always something new to learn and one needs to keep himself updated throughout his life. The day I lose the fire which motivates me to prove myself as a trainer is the day for me to say adios amigos to my profession.

Excuse me sir, May I have a minute or two?

When I turned, I found, Bharat standing behind me with a puzzled face. He continued by requesting me to help him in couple of other subjects which he was finding very troublesome. There was a silence in the room for a moment. "Why did he come to me knowing that I do not handle those subjects?" I wondered. He must have felt that the teaching techniques are effective and result driven. His confidence on me compelled me to say yes. I didn't mind putting a bit of extra efforts to live up to the faith he had on me. Every day I used to do my homework, just to make sure that I deliver my best in those two subjects that I have agreed to teach. Slowly, the number of students coming to me with favors increased and every time I had to do a lot of extra work at home.

My knowledge and capability to teach several subjects became my strength as well as my weakness.

Criticism comes only to those who perform. Who would rate a flop show? I feel that people who dare to be different are most talked about.

How can one person teach multiple subjects?

Is this a strategy to fetch more money from the students?

Questions like this rose on my proficiency but I only looked at the happy faces of my students whom I helped by burning midnight oil.

12 years ago, students came up to me for demo classes before they could decide that I will be able to teach them or not. Today, even after achieving such glory and success in this field, the scene remains the same as it was in the past. Demo classes are still going on to prove my effective teaching abilities.

Till date, I go back to my books and do my home work before I enter the class as I cannot afford to disappoint my students.

The confidence and conviction that my students have on me is my most prized possession.

28

Education + Career

Education became my career and I realized that teaching is my destiny. Being a true companion and paving a path for my students; a path which is ahead of me is my intention. Seeding the same amount of interest for Mathematics and Economics as I have among my students is my purpose.

Chirag Mehta, one of the brightest students of Karmasthali brought a new turn to my career. A shy boy who spoke rarely in the class but had amazing grasping power! His elder sister took Economics classes from me and scored extremely well. So, it was as clear as a bell that he joined Karmasthali too. He did not mind spending extra hours in class just to make sure that all his doubts are clear. He took accounts classes from Dipesh Sir who had his own educational institution named "Education + Career".

"Sir, Why don't you join "Education + Career" with Dipesh sir? There are more students over there who are willing to study from you", Chirag said to me.

That was my first rendezvous with Dipesh Majithia, Niladri Motilal and Surojit Singh, three wizards, all of them ruling the market in their respective fields. Once they introduced themselves, I felt as if I was like a toad which never comes out of the well.

Several styles of administration, teaching with different class strengths, scheduling the batches, different teaching methodologies, approached to be followed to handle students with different skills and mindsets and I learnt everything over a period of time with their assistance.

"Students will always remain students"

This became a common phrase amongst us. No matter how much you devote yourself for the students, you cannot expect anything in return from them.

If they pass, it is because of their own capabilities.

If they fail, it is because of the teacher.

In this industry, *the more the publicity the more the popularity!*

As a teacher, I always thought that my students will understand that whatever I say is for their own benefit. But I was wrong. The moment this toad (me) came out of the well, he understood that he is just a Joker whose job is to assist like a catalyst to a chemical reaction. Gone are the days when students obey their teachers. In generation next, if you wish to survive and maintain your stature then you will have to sell your skills. You got to prove that you can provide something better from the rest and you can perform.

"In order to survive in a world of instinct,
its' alternative is to hunt or being hunted.
Reject this, then be prepared to be hunted."
—*Toba Beta, My Ancestor Was an Ancient Astronaut*

29

Shree Krishna Avatar

Godfather, a mystical word—understanding which is beyond my capacity

After all, where did this word come from?

Does he play the role of a creator or a destroyer?

Avatar is a Hindi word which symbolizes "Manifestation of supreme power or deity in human body".

Shree Krishna is a divine being, the almighty, all knowing and all powerful. He is the originator of all forms of knowledge and fulfils all wishes of his devotees since time immemorial.

Heard a lot about Mohan Sir. Tales of his teaching styles were spread like forest fire in the market among Mathematics students. A part of me was jealous and other part felt motivated thinking that if I follow his footsteps then people will acknowledge me as well. But I wanted to implement his lessons in my own style. Never thought that, I will ever get a chance to meet him.

Just like Eklavaya, I was *unofficial* prodigy of supreme Guru "Dronacharya" nurturing myself and polishing my teaching methodologies.

I had never dreamt of face to face encounter with him but one day he appeared in front of me just like Lord Krishna.

After finishing Economics class in Education + Career, Dipesh introduced me with a gentleman saying "Sir, he is Mohit" and then slowly whispered in my ear, "He is the one, Mohan Sir". Mixed emotions exploded inside me, I was very nervous and happy at the same time.

He asked, *"What chapters can you teach in Mathematics and Statistics?"*

I replied, "Sampling theory is my favourite."

"Can you teach trigonometry?"

Yes, I said.

Ok. Then come to my centre tomorrow at 4 PM.

That day's 4pm and today's 4pm, its being 7 years now and still I worship him like Eklavya worshiped Guru Dhronacharya, the supreme guiding light, the master of masters.

The way Guru asked Eklavya to cut off his right thumb in honour of his teachings, may be, somewhere, even I had to give gratuity in obeisance to Mohan Sir. And that gratuity was a moral, a lesson, a message, an advice, I got everything without asking for it, I understood everything without hearing anything. The way Guru Dronacharya said to Eklavaya, "Cut off your right thumb. You cannot be the best at archery. No one could compete in Archery with my favourite and most accomplished student, Arjun".

Like a sincere student, he happily cut off his right thumb without even an ounce of pain on his face. Even I cut off my thumb in honour of my Supreme Guru, Mohan Sir.

One day he asked me if I like Economics more or Mathematics. He asked me to leave teaching one of the two subjects, either Mathematics or Economics. I replied,

"You have put me into a difficult situation. This is like choosing between your mother and wife. Both are integral part of your lives and you cannot imagine living without them."

He said nothing but had a sheepish smile on his face. Slowly, he made me away from both, my mother (Mathematics) and my wife (Economics) and asked me, what kind of a man was I. Neither was I able to handle my Mother nor my Wife.

After all, He was my Godfather. I reached heights of glory in teaching field only because of him. How could I disobey him? He asked me to become a Joker as this industry demands and I happily became one. He trained me to be polite, intelligent yet dumb and down to earth; every quality that a Joker must possess.

I became a Joker, because I wanted to learn.
I became a Joker, because it was important to be one.
I became a Joker because I had to entertain the audience.

I became a Joker to defeat that 'Arjun'!

I have not committed any mistake by becoming a Joker. Until and unless someone is sitting on your head with a stick, you do not finish your pending tasks. Isn't this like being an insane Joker? Being a Joker is not a mistake. If you wish to learn new skills, then be foolish, be hungry for success and be ready to erase old concepts from your mind to be able to start afresh.

The new twist in the story came when I was asked to mock him or substitute him for a session. Everything got changed after that session.

30

Prove me you know how to teach!

No one likes replacements or substitutes. Once we are accustomed to certain things, changes make us feel awkward. We take time to accept these changes in our lives and sometimes even after trying we are unable to accept them. For example, you are staying in a house for several years and suddenly because of some circumstances you have to change your city, location and home. Wouldn't you feel awkward initially? It is very human to feel uncomfortable upon encountering new people, new things and new places.

We hate changes in our lives. But we do not even realize that when do we eventually start loving them.

Mohan Sir: I will not be able to take class today as I have some work. You take the class as a replacement teacher and let us see how it goes.

Me: But Sir, You have been teaching them for so long. Will they accept this sudden change?

Mohan Sir: Do not worry about all that. Just take the class and do not scold students much. These students need to be handled with patience.

Me: As you say Sir.

Mohan Sir along with the head of the training centre sat on the last bench as the class started so that they could decide whether I am able to teach the students properly or not.

During the lecture, they got up and left the classroom. I paused for a second wondering why they left the class in between and then continued my lecture.

After the class, I asked the head that why did they get up in between the lecture and leave the classroom. He diplomatically replied, "We thought that your lecture was fine so we left the room."

Mohan Sir had to catch a flight that day for some personal work. Once he reached airport, he called me and said,

In reality, you have received negative feedback. Your performance was not up to the mark. Students did not like your way of teaching. That is why we left the room. Now, do as I say and follow my guidelines so that this will not be repeated from tomorrow.

Sadness clearly reflecting through my voice, I said, "Ok Sir, I will do what you feel is correct."

I became a marionette of his hands and did everything what he told me to do because I considered him my Godfather. Eventually, I realized that there exists no such thing such as 'Godfather'. Only with our own sincere efforts and dedication can we rise in our career. No one else can help us.

In this world, there exists God and there exists father but there is no such thing as Godfather.

I became a 'performer' who performs to the tunes of audience. Every time, I was given a new batch of students, I tuned myself up to get in sync with the students.

My students, who initially gave negative feedback about my teaching, slowly started loving me. There was a special and unique quality in me, which helped me to climb the ladder of success. I readily accepted the challenge whenever someone asked me, to *prove myself in teaching.*

There is absolutely nothing wrong in showcasing your skills for the contentment of your students.

In this field, there could be primarily two reasons for students to choose you as their mentor: **convenience** and **reference**.

Between these two factors, reference has more prominence.

If your work is good, people refer you and gradually your network expands.

Today I have 16 years of relevant experience in the market, 12 years in the teaching field and 4 years in sales and marketing but I never turned down my students whenever they asked me to give demonstration class.

Our downfall occurs when our Ego comes into picture. We should always keep our feet on ground no matter how high we rise in life.

Even after 16 years of experience, I never said, *"Do not ask me to prove how to teach. I have been in the market for many years now and I have already proved myself several times before"*

Even if I am the best trainer in the market, if I pass such a statement, students would rather prefer my competitors; who are still ready to win faith of their students in them by showcasing their skills and abilities to teach.

My suggestion to all youngsters who wish to enter this industry is never say, *"Do not ask me to prove how to teach".*

Always accept challenges with open arms and say, *"I can prove how to teach".*

31

The Magical Joker

One evening, sitting on my swing chair, I thought . . .

Who am I?

After self introspection for several hours, I came to a conclusion that . . .

I am a service provider; I am a Joker

Life of a service provider could be compared to the Joker card. A special playing card that trumps all others . . .

The Fool's card
A card that could change the game
A card of opportunity
The Imperial Bower
The Magician

The joker would not let one feel its presence but come as a saviour when one loses other cards. It allows the players to make a powerful combination which increases the chances of winning the game.

The joker card is no card but yet it is any card in the deck. It cannot be compared to other cards in the deck. It is flexible enough to form the personality of any card and yet has no personality of its own. This is what separates it from other cards. That is what makes it so special. It can prove to be bliss or a bane depending on the way it is used.

The joker is capable for impersonating any character with ease. It fits in everywhere. This is one of the most impressive traits of the Joker's personality. He accepts challenges and performs each of his acts with utmost perfection. Extremely independent by nature, the joker is full of creativity and positive spirit.

Life is a pack of 52 cards. It is an unsolved mystery. No one can predict the cards that life is going to give us. All we can do is to be a smart player and win the game of life. The Joker card might not be given importance initially but it knows how to make us realize its value.

Never take the Joker for granted, you never know when it might bring a twist in the game.

Who is a service provider?

A service provider plays a very significant role in our lives as we rely on the services provided by him in some way or the other. He knocks our door wearing a uniform, tie, shiny polished shoes and of course, a pleasant smile. Most of the times, we do not like his presence failing to realize that we all depend on him (may be directly or may be indirectly).

Irrespective of different needs and temperaments of the clients, the service provider never fails to please his customers who expect 24/7 availability, security, warranty, reliability, support, efficiency, value for money and quick resolution for every service they pay for. The service providers strive to achieve excellence in all these aspects only for one objective, Customer Satisfaction. For them, Customer is the King. But the customers cannot estimate the kind of efforts that these people put in to achieve fineness and quality.

The service providers play the same role in our lives as the Joker card in a deck of 52 cards.

But

Is there anything wrong in being a Joker?

Being a joker is nothing to be ashamed of. The joker can do wonders. It proves itself when people least expect it.

Yes, I am a Joker and I choose to be one!

I am a salesman, and I choose to be one!

I am a service provider, and servicing is fun.

I am a Joker, the 53rd card

Don't take me for granted, I am powerful and forward

I have my powers, I can change slot.

Till I bow down, and offer what I got.

Yes, I am a Joker and I choose to be one.

I am a service provider and I choose to be one.

The Magical Joker—Designed by Jyoti Ahirwar

DIAGONAL

Hi! I Am Amita

32

Sir, you don't worry!

Tring Tring. The phone on the other side kept ringing for a while and I was wondering in anticipation that whether this time I would be able to find one or not. Toiling over emails, e-chats and phone numbers, it was nearly more than three months and I was not getting a single person to help me with the transcription part of the tale. While the phone was ringing, I was eagerly waiting for it to be picked up.

I actually cursed the gentleman a couple of times who passed on the telephone number to which I had just now placed the call. There was finally a change in my cold behaviour once I heard, "Hello".

'Hello. Is this Amita?'

'Hi! I am Amita.'

That very answer secured me and made me think that finally I have found someone who is professional enough to introduce herself on asking, whether she is Amita or not. As on not so professional grounds, the pre judged answer from the other side would have been, yes! Who are you? Simply answering 'Yes' to any question is completely unprofessional according to me.

I started explaining the whole concept to her and there was complete silence from the other end. I thought whether she is even listening to me or not. I said: Are you there?

She politely responded "Yes, sir, I was listening, analyzing and trying to understand the whole idea. I have jotted down all the points and I was imagining how to put them across on a piece of paper in an artistic and influential manner." She then rephrased the entire concept to me and I was surprised with her enthusiasm and eagerness to take up this project.

She volunteered to put across her own ideas and said to me "Sir, I love writing. Writing is my passion. I would love to grab an opportunity which allows me to articulate my thoughts and emotions. You don't worry. This task is my responsibility."

I looked for such kind of a promise for a long time and her words gratified my hunger for assurance.

On the other hand, I doubted if she only knows how to blabber or she will actually reach up to my expectations. I asked her to do the groundwork for the topic given to her in a few words and told her that I will provide her with the feedback on that.

To be honest, I was not expecting much work to be done on the very first day. Next morning, when I woke up I was surprised to see an email in my Inbox with an attached file containing the work assigned to her.

After reading the file, I realized that she not only listened to me carefully but also embodied my experiences in specific formats as I asked her to do. In her work, she pointed out the missing links between the expectations of students and teachers while beautifully articulating the emotional aspect of their journey.

Her writing was not perfect but I could make out that every single word came straight from her heart.

I expected her to write only the summary on the first day, but instead she nearly finished a whole chapter!

And thus our journey to 'Four Corners of The Circle' started and soon I realized that with the efforts that she was putting into the work, I would soon be able to accomplish my dream of writing a book on my experiences.

My quench of being heard was gratified when I found someone who had the vision and patience to understand my emotions and express them with the same intensity.

I felt as if my soul was screaming for a long time:

Is anyone there?

Can anyone hear me?

I heard a voice saying "I am here, Sir" and I was convinced that yes, this is the person whom I have been looking for.

It is possible that I could have found writers who were better than her in terms of experience and vocabulary but I am certain of the fact that the spark I saw in her made her the chosen one. I saw a girl in her who wanted to break free and make her mark in this world.

Writing a book might not be a feat for some people, but for her it was a dream of her life. The best part is she did not know that I could foresee her dreams which will soon become a reality. She thought that she has to pen down my life on a piece of paper and she would be nothing but a ghost writer. I wanted to give the joy of writing to someone who values it; someone who has the same love of this book that I have; someone for whom it is not just a book but '**An opportunity of a Lifetime**'.

33

What Sets Us Apart!

Every Morning the first thought that pops up in my mind once I wake up is about '**Four Corners of The Circle**'. Once I close my eyes, all I could see is the day when our book will be published ready to inspire students with a hope that if it could set astir even one tenderfoot then my purpose of being a mentor will be met in its true sense.

Through this book, I want to give the most priceless gift to my students; the vision to excogitate the four corners of the circle.

I knew from the beginning that it would not be easy and I will have to cross many hurdles before I could reach my destination.

My intention is not to take out the frustration of my failures or boast about my success but to be able to bring about a refinement in the notion of students as well as educational institutes regarding post graduate professional courses, like for an instance MBA.

I was acquainted with the fact that this cannot be achieved in a day. It might not be Herculean for me to address what I want, to the audience; the real task was to make them hear what *I want to say not what they choose to understand.*

The first step of my trial was to make Amita understand that this book is not a biography; it is all about the four corners of the circle. To her, my words sounded ambiguous and confusing as since childhood she has been studying that the circle has no corners. I could not blame her for her counteraction. May be, if I was at her place, I would have reacted in the same manner.

Amita: "Sir, What are you saying? Your words are going above my head."

Me: "No need to understand anything for now. The day you will be writing the last page of this book is the day when you will realize the true meaning of the phrase '*four corners of the circle*'"

There was a silence for a few seconds at her end. I gave it some time, after which I started sharing my opinion about MBA and the conversation went on for hours. I began by telling her the name of the first chapter of the book "**One should not do MBA**". Hearing such a statement from a Management trainer was shocking for her. I continued my statement by saying that if the only reason people do an MBA is to get a better job or salary then one should not do MBA. She strongly agreed with me when I said that the only purpose of doing MBA should be to gain knowledge about different aspects of Management Skills. As a Teacher, I shared my experiences and discussed what kind of pressures students go through and what kind of guidance, understanding and support they expect from their teachers and parents.

The book is neither biased towards students nor educational institutes; the sole purpose is to provide their individual perspectives and reach to a common conclusion.

I feel that the only way the educational system can be made more productive is when teachers and students have an open discussion regarding what they expect from one another.

Amita had already started working on the book based on our discussion. As I expected, her write-up explained the challenges faced by the students to survive in the rat race and those faced by teachers wanting to impart knowledge.

The only thing which I found missing was **Structure** and **Format**. Though I loved her work but if it was not put across in a systematic manner, all her efforts will be wasted. She was expecting appreciation for her endeavours but instead I scolded her for not giving an order or a structure to the write up. At first she was downhearted by my remarks but she took it up as a challenge and dedicated all her efforts in improving the same.

After completion of the first chapter, we both had the satisfaction that we have been successful in describing the first corner of the circle.

When we moved on to the second topic, I told her about my journey as a school going student, college youngster and finally as a teacher. She could feel my pain of being misunderstood by the students for whom I struggled day and night only to make them successful in life.

Slowly, we both developed an immense respect for the book which made us give our best in order to make it happen. This is the best thing to happen in our life because for me it is about sharing my life experiences and for her; it is a beautiful dream; dream of becoming an author.

Finding out devoted time for the book out of busy schedule was a real challenge for me as well as for Amita. However, it is rightly said that nothing and no one can stop you from reaching your destination if you are determined and focused. No matter how difficult it was to manage time, our commitment, enthusiasm and zeal made it possible for us to give dedicated time to the book.

One day she called me and said: Sir, all I have in my life is work. I don't have any personal life. People find happiness by socializing or hanging out with friends. I find happiness in writing this book. I get goose bumps thinking of the day when this book will actually be published in the market.

I could feel the sadness in her words along with the undying passion to become a successful author. Through this book, I want to say the things which are unsaid and unheard. I want to give something to the young students, which is worth reading.

I started planning how I can make this dream come true. Does it involve only writing? I think it needs a lot more. Not only had I had to manage my time but also my finances and execution of publishing and marketing of the book.

There are millions of books in the market which talk about self-experiences but what sets our book apart from the rest?

Our life revolves in circles and we all are trying to find the corners. This book will help its readers find the four corners of a circle. Amita is a *diagonal of this circle* which connects the different corners and I am the centre of this circle where all corners meet.

34

Token of Appreciation

Be prepared for creating Four Corners of The Circle. Get geared up for the upcoming chapters of the Book, I said to Amita.

She replied, "Sure Sir. And I guess I would get the first copy of this book."

I acknowledged her words by saying, You will not ask me to give you the first copy of the book once you see the mail I just sent to you now.

Excited and nervous at the same time, she insisted me to tell her what the email was all about.

You will jump on your couch after reading it, I replied.

Exactly after two minutes I get a call from her, "Oh my God! Is this really going to happen? I don't believe this. Are you really going to add my name in the book? I never expected this. In fact, it is my dream to be known as an author. The cover page of the book having my name as the co-author is the most wonderful surprise that I have ever received in my life."

I was delighted after seeing her reaction to the token of appreciation that I gave to her. I controlled my beguilement and firmly said; now stop celebrating and get back to work.

Teamwork is very important for achieving maximum results. For an example; behind every successful film is a director, producer, music composers, singers, dialogue writers, actors, hair dressers, makeup artists, cameramen, spot boys and many more.

On screen, everything looks so fascinating and glamorous but in reality making a film involves a lot of hard work and efforts. Be it script writing, music composition, dubbing, promotion, production or direction, each and every part of film making is crucial to its success.

Similarly for every project, the work is divided among different people according to their skill-sets in order to bring it to a successful completion.

Making this book fortuitous will not be possible without her support and efforts. Introducing her as a co-author of the book is a small way of saying thank you to her.

With our commonsensical and impassionate approach towards the book, we were able to cover a substantial part in a few days after which I gave her a second surprise.

Guess what could it be? The epiphany was "Hi, I am Amita".

A plethora of emotions that we went through while articulating each chapter, the challenges that we faced to make it happen and how we overcome them, I wanted to capture everything.

Sitting on my chair, I went down the memory lane, the day when I wrote the book for the first time. While I was thinking of the heartache that I went through when the book which I had written with my soul, my heart was published in the name of some well-known author, Small drops of tears rolled down my cheeks.

I formed a love relationship with that book; love wherein I penned down all the theories that I had discovered throughout my career. Not getting recognition for the book to which I gave a part of myself was a setback for me. Innumerable copies of the book have been sold in the market today. I found my name only in the third last line of the acknowledgement section of the first edition of the book. Sadly, that too was replaced by someone else in the second edition.

How could I make someone else go through the same agony when I know how it feels when someone else takes credit for the work that you have done?

If Amita can help writing the book wholeheartedly without any expectation of being acknowledged then why can't I make a small contribution in making her career brighter by giving her appreciation for what she deserves? Giving wings to the dreams of that little girl makes me feel content.

~ A single act of appreciation or recognition could change some one's life.

35

Day Dreaming

People say that day dreaming is harmful and it cuts you off from the real world but I believe that it gives you the power to think out of the box, break rules and follow what your heart says to you is right. Anything wished from heart combined with genuine efforts to make you worth for it will be achieved sooner or later.

I normally woke up at 6 am in the morning to get started for the day full of challenges. Every day is a new beginning, a new demur and some milestone to be achieved.

Before going to college, I would read the entire book and try to analyze how can I make it better? When I say better, I mean, I want to know how I can make the readers understand what I really want to say.

At a point in my life, my dreams were left in the lurch. This book has brought a transition in my life by bestowing me dreams of eminence and ardour that fuel my impulse and vision of life.

I caught myself smiling a couple of times thinking about the book which embodies my journey in a nutshell. These magical day dreams glorify my self esteem. They guide me to sail in a new direction, rekindle the spark within me and drive my actions in a favourable demeanour.

While discussing about the book, Amita said "I know this is not going to be easy. In fact, anything great cannot be achieved without putting consistent and dedicated efforts into it. I do not want to think how it can be done; I just know that it has to be done. When something gives you happiness, no matter how many obstructions might occur in the path, nothing and no one could stop you from achieving it. I have even started day dreaming about this book"

I felt as if she spoke my heart out. "Almost everything that a human mind can imagine can be turned into a reality." I replied.

She further added "Sometimes, I pen down my thoughts on a piece of paper, sitting on my comfortable cushion; gazing at the moon. The cool breeze blowing away the vibrant red curtains in the spotless milky white room making me feel divine. Within a few hours, the golden light of the dawn hits the room, giving me a sense of joy being one among the very few to have a glimpse of the dazzling sun."

I could feel how much the dream of becoming an author matters to her. When you have an immense desire within you, you do not even feel the pain of thorns pricked while you are walking towards your goal. All you could see is your dream; all you could feel is the happiness of its fulfilment!

This book is not a semi-biography; it contains a life. It is about the struggle of a man from his childhood, school life, graduation days, post-graduation days and finally as a trainer. Someone who is trying to figure out who he actually is? Is he a poet, a mentor, an author, a speaker or a consultant? It is his fight against the designs; his mission of finding out four corners of the circle. His hope of reaching to people and voice out his opinions!

36

Yes, we will have the book launch in Bangalore

One fine day, after I finished narrating one of the incidents of my college life, she said to me, "Sir, I am in Bangalore and you are at Kolkata but I want to be present at the launch of our book. May be, I will start saving at least a month in advance so that I could book my flight to Kolkata."

Do not worry; the launch party of the book will happen in Bangalore itself, I said.

She was rejoiced at my statement of having the book launch ceremony in Bangalore.

Different authors feel different about the publishing of their book after several years or months of effort. I go through a surfeit of emotions when I think of the book signing day. A part of me is flying high and a part of me is ambivalent as I still have to go through the grandiose grind of promotion.

"Will 1 lose my reason to be happy once our dream of "Four Corners Of The Circle" comes true?" Amita asked.

I replied; it is all up to you. Then, you need to discover new milestones to achieve, new challenges to overcome and a new reason to be zestful. This book marks the beginning of new felicities and accomplishments. It opens the doorway to splendour and exaltation.

Amita is among one of the few people who have the courage to walk in a dark direction. An unknown path, where you are uncertain if you will ever be able to reach the destination and the murkiness does not allow you see what comes in your way.

I do not know what's going to happen? Will our book be successful? One thing that I am sure about is that I will write this book straight from the heart irrespective of the outcomes. I added.

According to me, taking each moment as it comes is the best way to be happy. Sometimes not knowing what will happen in the future is the greatest motive force. Amita and I were walking on a mischievous path, unaware of the repercussions. And the best part is that we were free from the fear of failure. If at all, success comes to us through this book; it will be like a cherry on the cake.

Holding this book in my hand which has a crux of my life itself gives me a sense of extreme beatitude. When

Amita got to know she will be the co-author, she felt that this would be the greatest reward and she does not expect anything more than this.

Every time I close my eyes to take a nap, I see the day when this book will be introduced to the public. The few minutes that I would use to speak about the book while launching will be compelling as it could make or break the success of the launch party.

The very thought of the publishing of this book is heart-warming. For me, it will be successful if it is being sold in every local market, not just the book stores and shopping malls. It is a book for every student and his/her battle to prosper in life.

It will be the day when the purpose of my life will be achieved as the book contains the feelings, thoughts and emotions which are left unspoken and unheard.

37

Meet Amita
A Writer—An Author

"An author has readers. A writer doesn't"
Jason Stanford.

If you ask me, "Who is an author?" I would say—

An author is an architect who constructs a beautiful house of words in which several emotions like love, passion, antagonism, regret, resentment, fear, anger, cheerfulness and enthusiasm coexist.

An author can also be compared to a painter who fills a canvas with beautiful colours using a palette of his wisdom.

An author is a mirror who introduces one to self. An author is a teacher who prepares you for a better tomorrow.

And I want you to be all of these, I said to Amita.

This book is like a magic wand, which brought a metamorphosis in her life.

Every one of us is a writer at some or the other point in our lives. We write notes, school papers, prepare lists, emails, letters and so on but being an Author has a much deeper meaning.

An author is praise worthy if after reading the book you feel that you know him very closely and you feel connected to whatever you read.

The wordsmith always keeps in mind that the world is going to read the ideas and experiences expressed in his/her work and every single word used in it needs to be chosen carefully.

Amita: Sir, at times, I research for several hours for a single thought that is expressed in this book as words hold power to influence the lives of the people in many ways. I would take care that this book gives a hope to the readers. A hope that they can be one amongst those who have achieved something in their life.

Words are wonderful . . .
Words are powerful . . .
And they can make or break someone's life.
So each word in this book would be the chosen one.

Me: Sometimes, two words have the same meaning but it is an art of an author to decide what the best way to put across a thought. For Example; I want to say that he failed the examination because he did not study. That is how an ordinary person would frame this sentence.

On the contrary, an author would say instead:

It is certain that he would have surely cleared the examination if he made a conscious effort to prepare for it.

The first and the second sentence nearly have the same meaning. However, the former sentence would make the reader feel unhappy. On the other hand, the latter sentence would give readers a hope that if he had studied, he would have cleared the examination.

The job of an author is to inspire his readers. To be able to create positive statements, an author has to be a positive human being in his personal life as well. If he is dull and unhappy, he would not be able to reflect positivity in his writing as well.

Amita: We want our readers to think positive and I would try my best to create a positive impact on their minds. It does not matter if I have to rewrite the entire content, but the end result should be positive.

Me: Good. I expected the same answer from you.

This was one of the conversations that we had while the book was in the making.

It is important for an author to be able to convey the intended message through his/her writing. No matter how refined a person's writing might be, if he/she is unable to put across the desired idea, it is meaningless.

While one is reading this book, they should feel that I am talking to them. It should be a reflection of me, I said to Amita.

It is my responsibility to convey your thoughts to the world, she replied.

She always made sure that she wrote my mind. She has the ability to be in someone else shoes' and pen down their real emotions. This is one of the most appreciable qualities in her.

Worried about the promotion of the book I asked Amita, Have you thought how we are going to promote this book?

Do not worry Sir. My family, school friends, college buddies, office colleagues, teachers, relatives, friends of friends, family friends, relatives' friends, all of them are going to read this book. They would itself make a count of at least 1000. By that time, the book would be already popular and everyone else will also read it, she answered.

I was amused at her reaction but I appreciated the spirit and positivity in her regarding our book.

Through our journey, I wanted to see the changeover of Amita from a *Writer* to an *Author*. I have already experienced the excruciating pain of not being able to enjoy the success of my efforts and the credit for my work being taken by someone else which makes me feel that even my enemies do not deserve this. Every time I saw that book in a store or someone carrying it, I wanted to scream out loud:

Hey, I am the one who wrote this book but a different name on the cover page stopped me from doing so.

Every time someone spread word of mouth about that book stating

It is a must read . . .
Good book . . .
Well written . . .

I felt as if someone stabbed my heart.

I didn't want Amita to become another Mohit Jain. She was an unpolished gem, I wanted her to nurture self and stand in front of the world in such a way that no one could point out at me regarding my decision of choosing her.

The only reason I pointed out even the slightest of the mistakes that she committed was to see significant improvement in her thought process, vocabulary, creativity and sentence formation as the book progresses.

Initially she might felt bad on my reprimanding her, but then she will have to go out of her way to bring more maturity in her writing.

At times, I would knock her down shrewdly just to make sure that I could bring out the emotions so that same could reflect in her writing.

You have to walk an extra mile to cover the journey between a writer and an author. I do not care about your work schedule. If I want the content to be completed, I want it to be completed. I am not interested about your personal life and do not give me any excuses for the delay, I said to her once and she broke down.

The only intention behind this was to bring out the seriousness and commitment towards the work that we were doing together.

The next day onwards, I see a complete transformation in her approach towards the book. I cannot say that she was not doing well initially. At times, I forced myself to be shrewd even after knowing that she will be hurt but my intention was to keep her focused and aligned. She started finding out ways to improve her skills as a writer. I could see tremendous improvement in her writing style, language and of course meeting the deadlines.

Today, I can proudly say, "Meet Amita, An Author."

SQUARE

FIFTH Corner of the Square

F	I	F	T	H
FUN	IMAGING	FASHION	THEORY	HOPES

38

JUICE Mantra

The foundation of success depends upon how profoundly you have been using the JUICE Mantra in your day-to-day life. To delve into the vast scope of education, one should constantly strive to emerge as better. By being 'better' I hint at developing interpersonal skills, prowess to think what is appropriate and how much one is ready to trade-off.

Nothing is available free of cost. The supreme power on this earth is money. The more you have the more powerful you are.

You cannot walk if you cannot see. You need to visualize things with an open mind if you want to succeed in life. If you keep your eyes closed, you will be stuck, you will not reach anywhere.

The ultimate goal of life is to reach heights which can be realized only by visualizing things. For a frog in a well the world is very small, he will realize that the world is beautiful only if he jumps out of the well.

Only an open eye can see things clearly. Unless, you see a thing, you cannot describe it and here visualization plays a very vital role.

By visualizing, you will be able convey your point across in a powerful and compelling form.

Virtual Imaging is something like finding an eye for a deaf and an ear for a blind.

If you want to be successful, you just can't stop here. Ask yourself, what is the trend of being successful? Simply following the current fashion will help you gain momentary satisfaction but in the long run, when fashions will keep changing now and then, what would you do? Develop skills to implement new trends in your work. Be trendy in terms of ideas. Create your own style statement. I follow my fashion trends and manage them too.

The overall picture of what I am, what I want to be and what I want in the future can come alive or real if one tries to play the nine point game. It has been tested many a times and has always helped to improve the frame, the target and what all we require to achieve that target.

The last leg of my fifth corner lies in hopes. Finding opportunities in the lost world, the scenes from where we have moved on. If you can master the way to deal with something which is lost, you have the foundation—the fifth corner foundation. And on this fifth corner, stand tall, is our resolution to energize the youth, and bring back JUICE into our lives.

Let us build the square with a fifth corner!

39

Fun is Free, but not Lunch!

Nothing is for free.

Money rules the world. The more one has, the more powerful one is.

It is very easy to pass such a statement, but . . .

What are we running for, all through our lives, **Success**!

Yes, it is true, we all run for it but hidden truth behind it is *Money*. Most of us might not want to agree with this point. Everyone says that they need success but in reality they are looking for 'Financial' success. I would want to take a very simple but real example. When one starts career, one has great and innumerable dreams.

That big car, That luxurious home, Leisure time at that place!

We all enjoy Panipuri/Golgappa at the corner street, but cross your heart and say would you want to continue that throughout your life?

It is fun but only once in a while, not every day.

We want to reach the heights of success, only one reason being, "Nothing is free".

Be it fun, be it leisure time.

Be it accessorizing our self.

In one way or another, we must pay.

Leisure time with family will cost productive time.

Fun, outings or amusement parks, everything costs money. It is a very debatable point to say that "Nothing is for free".

Think, think deep inside, in one way or another, we spend something to get something.

It is a fact of life. The barter system is what we have learnt from nature.

If one needs something, one needs to give something in exchange. It might not be mandatory, but we all must spend. We all must spend our childhood to learn. We must spend time to have fun with family. We must spend our energy, skills and talent to succeed in our career so on so forth.

Having said that, "yes, nothing is for free!"

What are we referring to here?

We all strive to succeed no matter what we spend in some way or the other.

Again, simple example which is more common in our lives, If we had to travel from one part of the city to another, let us say, MG Road to Richmond town in Bangalore via taxi, it would take approximately 5 minutes but would cost minimum 200 rupees.

If we take auto rickshaw, it would take 20 minutes and cost us less than half of it.

If we walk, it's free but would take nearly 45 minutes.

What I mean to say is *Time Costs Money*.

Last weekend, I went to a grocery shop to purchase some household items. My eyes stopped at a ceramic plate labelled as 'unbreakable' with a price tag of 50 rupees. I thought How could an unbreakable plate cost rupees 50? I took the plate and smashed it on the floor. Everyone in the shop gave me those deadly looks as if I am a hardcore criminal who just ran away from the jail. To my surprise, it was indeed unbreakable. There was not even an inch of damage to the plate. As I went through different sections of the shop, I came across this royal and exquisite glass plate which was also labelled as 'unbreakable'. This time the price tag was rupees 699. I immediately believed that it would be.

Our perspective of seeing things changes when they have a higher value.

Have you ever felt that you initially disliked a movie or song but after constant promotion, you eventually started liking it, in fact loving it? That is the magic of promotion.

What I mean to say is, if you increase your value, the way, people look at you will change.

How can you increase your value?

Let us talk about time and value. If I want to learn something, either I need to spend more time with less money or less time with more money. For example, crash courses, they just run. Fast, but cost more, same course, provided on a slow pace costs less.

What more to say? Time costs money but it even depends on our skill set. We cannot buy everything for money. Some things are priceless. Knowledge is one such bliss which could help one to go forward in life even with lesser investment of money. A student who has a hunger of success would study even without proper facilities and world class training. Knowledge, talent and skills are such pure virtues which cannot be bought. It has to come from within. It is the 'inner voice' that decides the future of any person.

During our college days, most of us have a casual approach towards studies. We expect that we have given huge amounts of admission fee and we will get placement as a complimentary gift. But that is not true. The college will take initiative and responsibility of placing those students who have a good academic record throughout the course curriculum. We cannot expect that we would be offered a great job with several backlogs to clear.

College is providing your placement; you need to give them something in return too. And that something is 'efforts' and 'hard work'.

If these elements are missing within you, there is no point cursing the college for not providing good placements at the end.

One pays for the fees and not the placement. Job comes to you only if the employer feels that you could be a profitable resource to that company. In order to prove this, one must have good academic record, strong aptitude, correct attitude and communication skills. We need to increase our value so that we could change the way people see us.

In this modern era, we buy time by paying the price for it. Our parents spend money for our future, we spend our talent to grow and our family spends emotions to make sure that we stick together. We all have hurdles to reach the destination and in order to reach our goal; we have to pay the price.

Yes, it is true, hard fact of life, "Nothing is for free"

You need love; spend your emotions.
You need success; spend your talents.
You need a cure for disease; spend money.

And it is all up to us to define what we need and
For that we must spend

Nothing is for free!

40

---

*Virtual Imaging—An Eye for a
Deaf and an Ear for a Blind!*

How many of you find it difficult to communicate with
people you know?

Well, most of us are comfortable talking to people with
whom we are well acquainted.

Now, some questions arise in my mind:

- How many of you find it difficult to communicate
  with people who are unfamiliar to you?
- Have you experienced situations where you forget
  all the concepts that you have learned in front of
  the interviewer?
- Do you fumble while talking to a person for the
  first time?
- Does your heart race faster if you are asked to
  speak in front of people on a stage?

I am sure that the answer would be 'Yes' for most of us. It is a common behaviour to feel nervous while communicating with strangers.

Communication skills play a pivotal role in every sphere of life. Having knowledge is good but presenting it in an appropriate manner is important in order to get noticed among the crowd. Whether it is about cracking an interview, academic growth or promotion; communication skills are given a lot of prominence.

People who are incapable of communicating effectually at times suffer from inferiority complex and insecurity.

Now, how to overcome this fear of exchanging ideas with people who are unknown?

If there is no problem in communicating with the known; then is there any problem in communicating with the unknown?

Imagine a scenario where you are in a lecture room in which you rarely know anyone. You forget your pen at home and now you need it to be able to take notes. Will anyone harm you if you ask them for an extra pen?

They will either give you the pen or say that they do not have an extra one.

My point is if you are not saying anything wrong, then the person to whom you are talking would not kill you. Take this fear out of your mind thinking how would the other person react if you initiate talking to them?

In fact, most beautiful professional and personal relationships begin with small talks.

You never know that the person with whom you initiate a small talk could be your lifelong business partner or soul mate.

By putting across a question and answering it yourself, the solutions to most of the problems can be attained.

As it is said that every coin has two sides, similarly; the solutions that we are talking about here can be viewed from different perspectives.

- First solution is communicating effectively with people who are unknown to us or with whom we are conversing for the first time.
- Second solution is to do self examination by constantly talking to self.

Both these solutions have their positive and negative effects. However, rather than focusing on their demerits, here I would like to throw light on the positive results that these models can provide to us.

The two models are:

- **Virtual Imaging**
- **Talk to your Ghost**

Virtual Imaging

Framing pictures in mind of things that you want to happen in your life is the first step towards converting them into reality.

As the name suggests, virtual imaging is framing pictures in mind of things which do not exist in reality. This might sound outlandish initially, but if used in a correct way, it can help one to get over the fear of communicating with strangers.

Has this ever happened that the entire scene of an interview room comes in front of your eyes before you actually go for the interview?

We all have butterflies in our stomach before attending an interview. You can follow these steps which would help you to be confident during the interview.

1. Think of all possible questions than an interviewer might ask you like:

   - Tell me something about yourself.
   - Where do you see yourself five years from now?
   - What is your ultimate goal?
   - What is your expected pay package?
   - When you can join the company at the earliest, if selected for the post?

2. Contemplate and then frame answers to all these questions. Visualize the conversation.

3. Once you are prepared, you would be able to answer each question with ease. The reason being, if someone asks what your ultimate goal is, some people never really gave a serious thought to what they ultimately want to achieve in their lives. If they do mind plotting a night before an interview and then take proper sleep, they would know what to say.

4. After the interview, you can analyse if the questions you prepared were really asked? If yes, how did you perform? How can you make it better?

5. Even if the questions that you prepared were not asked in the interview, still you never know some other employer might ask you the same questions in future.

6. Prepare a list of all the questions that were asked. Frame answers for all of them. This is a good practice and can help you to crack an interview in future. You would have an idea, what questions are generally asked and what would be the appropriate answers for them.

7. Observe the body language, expressions, gestures and reactions of the person taking your interview. This would give you an idea whether the interviewer likes you or not and what are your chances of being selected.

To be able to efficaciously communicate with others, you first need to start talking to things that cannot respond to you.

This could actually make a huge difference in improving your communication skills. Let us take a daily life example:

You: Why do not you work, silly remote control? Tap tap (you hit the Television remote control twice)

You: Ah it works after hitting it twice on its head. May be, I need to change its batteries to make it work fine.

The Problem is solved.

When you talk to non living objects, you ask a question and you only give an answer for it. The reason is that you are thinking if it would have been a living being, how would it respond? You can implement the same thing while communicating with living beings as well. You can predict a response to your statement or question and then speak accordingly. This will not only help you to develop cordial relationships with your acquaintances and co-workers but also play a vital role in avoiding conflicts with them.

Virtual imaging is indeed an eye for a deaf and an ear for a blind. For a person who cannot see, his ears are the most powerful weapons as he can frame pictures in his mind by listening. Melody of early morning birds, resonance of rain drops falling on a window pane and the sounds of footsteps. Everything is magnificent for a person who is deprived of vision. Similarly, for a person who cannot hear, his eyes are his most valued weapons as he can hear things through his eyes.

Virtual imaging is one mighty weapon which allows you to overpower your weaknesses with your strengths.

Talk to your Ghost

Introspection makes life simpler.

An empty mind is a devil's workshop. But who is this devil?

This devil is no one else but your inner self, your ghost. We need to talk to our ghost to be able to discover ourselves. The word 'ghost' here implies our inner conscience. Just like we are scared of encountering ghosts, similarly we are scared to confront our inner conscience too. We tend to run away from our inner voice in the same way we run away from ghosts. The moment we gather courage to talk to our inner ghost, is the moment when we revive and a fresh new start will take place.

Let us take a daily life example in which one does self talk:

You pick a shirt or a dress and you look at the mirror and ask yourself how the outfit looks on you.

This helps you to choose a dress that suits you best. There are many such instances in which we talk to our inner self and get solutions for most of our problems.

Have you ever stood in front of the mirror while practicing a speech, a dance performance or even while studying?

Do this simple exercise and see if it helps you in any way:

Prepare a speech on a topic on which you would like to speak. For example; some change that you wish to bring in your country or some advice that you would like to give to the people.

Once the speech is prepared, stand in front of the mirror; hold the paper in which you have written the speech and start speaking.

Observe your body language, hand movements, gestures and expressions and think what impact your speech will create on the audience. Would you like if the same speech is given by someone else in the same way? How can you make it more powerful? What modulations in voice, hand movements, expressions or gestures can you make to express a particular emotion, thought or idea at its best?

After practicing the speech for a couple of times, put the paper aside.

Now follow the same procedure without referring to the paper.

This exercise would not only bring immense confidence in you but also help you to become a great public speaker. The reason is **you** are your truest companion and the mirror tells you things which others cannot. Talking to your inner self helps you to organize your thought process.

Listening to radio is the best way to relax. Don't you love how RJ's play with their voice. Can't you imagine the expressions on their face only by the tone or pitch of their voice? They entertain people only by making modulations in their voice. Isn't it great? Once you have the power to involve people in the conversation only by making variations in the tone and pitch of your voice, you become a good speaker in its real sense.

I still remember how our business communication professor made us do an exercise for enhancing our conversational skills. Each one of us was given a topic to speak on. The twist was that the speaker had to stand behind the screen and express his/her views on the topic. It was challenging for us to express each idea, thought and emotion only through our voice. My topic was "over smart jackass and a live wire". These were the two titles given to me by my college mates. Some considered me an over smart jackass and for some of them, I was as alert and active as a live wire. My heart raced, when my turn came. Trust me it was not as easy as I thought it to be. That day I realized playing with voice is indeed an art. I would say that it was an amazing learning experience.

Form a beautiful relationship with your inner self. Take a little time from your busy schedule, start questioning yourself and try to find answers to those questions. Be sure of what you know. If you want to distinguish between your living and existing, then start judging yourself rather than judging others.

For example, suppose you think that calculation and estimation are the same. If you think so then why do you think so? If this is not the same then why this is not the same? Start finding the reasons. You will reach to the correct answer.

Do not get satisfied with your answers. Keep on questioning. It will help you to get the best possible answer and with this practice you will get to know all the possible questions regarding a particular subject or matter.

Think whatever you want to think. Give free expression to your thoughts. Allow your thoughts to go in different directions. First collect your thoughts and then do not hesitate to scatter them. Unless you do this, you will not be able to think further. Let your ghost or spirit wander.

Tell your ghosts about your negative emotions or thoughts that you cannot tell anyone else. Tell your ghosts all the things you think you cannot do. It is not about putting yourself down. Once you start knowing negative things about yourself, you will start fulfilling prophecies out. You may fail or you may make mistakes but it will increase your chances to overcome your incapability.

So start imagining. Talk to the inner self. Talk to things that cannot talk. Talk to your ghost.

41

Fashion in Management—
Managing Fashion!

Fashion is how you think, not how you look!

What is fashion?

Different people define this term in different ways.

One day, I decided to ask this question to various people and see what they have to say about it.

What is fashion for you?

Here are a couple of answers that I got . . .

It is something which keeps changing.

Being classy and fabulous.

Keeping your heels and head high.

Being comfortable with oneself.

Gucci, Prada, Guess and Valentino.

It is a way of life.

Pretty interesting and different answers . . . .

After analyzing these answers, I came to a conclusion that

Fashion is attitude

As it is said, before leaving from home, do not forget to wear your smile and attitude.

Do biggest brands, shiny shoes, luxury cars, extravagant phones and opulent homes make one powerful and attractive?

Maybe yes.

Have you ever thought that what makes people like Amitabh Bachchan (India's greatest actor), Mahendra Singh Dhoni (India's cricket team captain) and Narendra Modi (political figure) so prosperous?

It all started from their vision, attitude and thought.

They had imagined their lives to be like this. Their thinking was fashionable and that has what made them fashionable.

These people do not have the best features, complexion or body, but when they walk, when they talk, they create a powerful impact.

If Amitabh Bachchan spreads a word of mouth about a product, no matter how overpriced or awful it might be, people will like it and buy it.

But he was an ordinary struggling actor at a point of time, whom no one even knew. What made him reach this far?

Is it his clothes, money or looks?

No, it is his attitude and thinking. It is his vision.

Of course, there can only be one Amitabh Bachchan. But there is only one you too. You cannot be like them but yes, you can create your own identity in your own way.

Become fashionable, stylish and attractive but by being yourself and not aping others.

Have you ever felt inferior about yourself because of your obesity, crooked teeth or short height?

May be you could turn it to your advantage and convert it into your most attractive asset. The ball is in your court. People will believe what you choose to show project yourself.

Most of the times, no one knows about flaws in your looks until you tell them.

How many times do you complain about the way you look, the way you talk, walk, think, eat and sleep?

Don't you wish to look like someone else?

How many times do you wish to swap life with someone else?

Every creation of god is beautiful and so are you. God has made everyone special in their own way and so are you. You are special. Realize this. Say to yourself every morning, I am beautiful/handsome and feel the difference.

Knowledge vs. Communication Skills has been a very debatable topic since the beginning.

What does an interviewer look for in an ideal candidate?

- Experience
- Knowledge
- Communication Skills
- Presentation Skills

It would be unfair to choose one among these. People who believe that knowledge is the key to crack any interview are right and those who believe that presentation or communication skills matter a lot are also right. Both knowledge and communication are equally important. But once you are entering into the industry, what will be the first thing people are going to look at?

A formally dressed person with correct body language and posture earns some golden points even before the interview starts.

It is not necessary to wear the most expensive attire in order to create a positive impression on the mind of the Hiring manager. Even with simple, neat, well ironed formal clothes, you can look presentable. But yes, relying completely on these factors is wrong.

At the end of the day, they would consider how modern, fresh and fashionable your ideas are.

Wonderful ideas would get you a job and not a wonderful face.

What is fashion in management?

In management, one has to sell himself first to be able to sell his products and services.

Have you ever walked out of a shop just because the shopkeeper did not attend you properly?

I am sure you would have. Similarly, has it ever happened that you purchased more items than what you had decided just because the seller provided excellent hospitality to you?

A seller can make his products or services look good or bad just by following the art of presentation. Highlighting the benefits or qualities of the products and camouflaging the flaws is in the hands of the seller.

Making customers believe that they are purchasing the right product from the right source depends on how you win their faith. Choosing the right words at the right time in the right situation is important.

How to manage your style?

The answer is simple. By creating your own identity; by knowing your potential.

The Chocó chip cookies which come in a ravishing packing are so popular and priced. Why?

Many companies focus on giving an attractive packing to their products so that they could lure the customers.

Don't you feel like owning the products that look tantalizing?

But yes, only packing won't help. After trying out the product, if the quality does not turn out to be good, it is certain that you will never purchase that product again.

Similarly, you have to pack yourself in an attractive form keeping in mind that packing would help only if the content is also good.

Only packing and no quality can be a disaster.

There is nothing wrong in getting inspired from the other's style statement but it is important to implement that in your own way.

There is a very thin line between getting inspired and copying some one's ideas. No one likes duplicate items. Everyone likes original ones. Do not try to become a duplicate of someone else. If you do so, people will always prefer the original version and you would lose your value.

People criticize everyone for everything. Changing self because of others criticism is nothing but proving them right.

Be yourself. Stay the way you are. If you are a bad singer then think that no one can sing as bad as you and that is what makes you adorable. If you are fat, you are. If you are short you are. Be proud of what you are. Do not change for others. Let people love you and not the mask that you carry on your face. Take off this mask and throw it away. Accept yourself and slowly people will start accepting you.

When people know about your accomplishments and struggle behind it, they will surely respect you but . . . .

When you are walking on the street, do people who are completely unfamiliar treat you with the same dignity and respect?

This can be accomplished if your eyes talk, your walk talks, your clothes talk, your shoes talk, in fact, even your spectacles talk about you . . . .

You should be able to communicate even without saying a single word . . . only by the way you dress, walk and talk.

Your expressions, body language, hand movements and gestures say a lot about you. A human being is capable of expressing every emotion only with the help of gestures and body language.

Confidence is reflected clearly on your face if you are a person of substance.

Fashion to me is respect.

- What kind of respect you want from others is just the mirror image of the kind of respect you give to others.
- Respect is something one needs to earn.
- Ask for respect, you will definitely get it. But one also needs to show that one is worth it.

42

The Nine Point Theory

The theory is simple. Below are the rules of the game '9 point theory':

•   9 points are given to you in the fashion shown in the picture given below.

•   Your task is to join these nine points with minimum number of straight lines possible without lifting your hand from the paper.

- A straight line can be horizontal, vertical or inclined at any angle.
- As you change the angle, the count of straight lines is incremented by one. Suppose you move horizontally and then you move vertically, it would be counted as two lines.
- You can move away your hand from the paper once you have joined all the nine points.

As the game starts, nearly everyone would think of joining these 9 points with five lines as shown below:

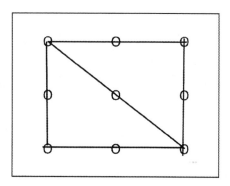

The reason being, this task can be completed with the given set of restrictions and rules using five lines in the most convenient and simple way.

When we enter the corporate world as a fresher or inexperienced, we tend to work according to the resources available to us under the given set of time and performance constraints.

It is a typical and natural for human beings to act like this. There is nothing wrong in completing this task with five lines as we have no prior knowledge or experience of the game.

Perfection comes with knowledge and experience. Expertise cannot be attained in a day. Time and patience is the key.

This task can be completed with 4 lines also as shown in the diagram given below:

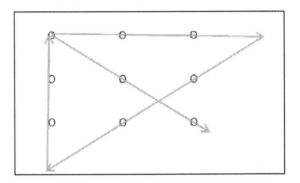

When I gave this task to my class with the strength of over 100 students, only a handful of students were able to execute the task within 4 lines because they were already aware of the game and practiced it before.

After a couple of attempts, most of the students were able to figure out how to consummate the same task within four lines.

On carefully observing the above figure, the two triangles symbolize two towers of strength; '*Market Expertise*' and '*Market Knowledge*'. With the help of these weapons, one can simplify the work carrying it out in a more efficient way and within a lesser time frame.

For example; a tenured employee is given Rupees 25,000 to do the same task which a fresher does in Rupees 10,000.

This is because an experience person would deliver the same work within the lesser amount of time. Also, his work would be flawless and more effective. Hence, he is paid more.

For any organization, time is money. For them, meeting deadlines and achieving customer satisfaction is the topmost priority.

The fastest performer you are, the more you are paid.

There are 10,000 ways of doing the same work. What matters is how you do it. If I now ask you to hold your ears, there are innumerable ways of doing so.

But the rule of the game is, *"The simpler, the better. The faster, the Master"*

Imagine if there was no time frame given to attempt a competitive examination, everyone would be able to clear it sooner or later. The master is the one who is able to solve each mathematical question correctly within one minute. Time is precious. Even if a student knows how to solve all the questions, it does not matter if he or she cannot solve it as quickly as one minute.

How do we make ourselves better?

As we get to know about number of our competitors and where do we stand among them, we prepare ourselves accordingly. If over 3 Lac students sit for an examination every year, the probability of cracking the exam becomes 1/300,000.

In order to beat 299,999 competitors, one needs to think out of the box and make extraordinary efforts. Only with consistent efforts and **out of box thinking** could lead them towards their goal.

"Think beyond your capacity in order to achieve beyond your expectations"

How far can you think to complete the given task in the simplest, fastest and most efficient manner?

The good news is that the same task can also be done with three lines as shown in the figure below:

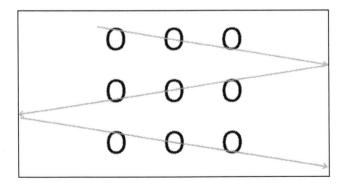

If the same work which is done by a fresher and a tenured agent is given to a general manager, how would he do it?

Whenever there are any issues in the organization, does a manager speak to every employee in order to sort it out?

No, he chooses a simple yet effective path by speaking to the representative or a team leader who knows everything about the team.

If we ask a general manager to join these nine points, he would treat each dot as an area of concern. The first line passes from the top of the first point, middle of second point and bottom of the third point. It then reflects and follows the reverse order. It again reflects and follows the original order. The problem is solved.

A general manager would need power to be able to do this. Now, where this power comes from?

It comes with years of experience, in depth knowledge and complete expertise.

From this theory, we draw following conclusions:

- With the help of industry exposure, knowledge and experience, one can perform his or her work more effectively and productively.
- To be able to reach the third level, one need to cross the first and second stage, only then he would be able to do justice to the third level. Only after joining the nine points using 5 and 4 lines will you be able to discover how to do it in three simple lines.
- Keep your expectations low. One has to enjoy the journey before reaching the destination. If you

say, that you have the knowledge and should be given the position of general manager directly. You would miss all the knowledge that an ordinary employee gains before he becomes a manager.

Once you become the general manager of the company what next and how? For reaching beyond this point, one needs to traverse the off beaten path. Life is magical. One simply needs to discover it.

And this task can also be done using one line . . . .

43

Hopes—Opportunities of Being Lost!

'LOST'—The very feeling of being lost ignites a multitude of emotions within us which are very diverse in nature. Some might be lost emotionally, spiritually or soulfully. In this world, we are all lost; each one of us is in search of something. Search is what keeps our lives running. It is a marathon which never ends. As a student, one searches for better academic options, as a breadwinner, one keeps searching for better career options and so on.

The feeling of being lost means something entirely different to a fresh graduate than what it means to a senior manager of a multinational company or to a tourist visiting a foreign country. However, the cardinal symptoms such as fear, insecurity or anxiety are common to the majority. The experience of being lost arouses within us a feeling of separateness, a state of being cut off from what we call as a normal life. Hence to be lost means to be helpless, unable to grasp the world—things and people—actively; it means that the world can invade us without our ability to react.

It's an accidental leap beyond our comfort zone. It is not unusual to feel lost while sitting in our own living room, might be for a minute or two but we all are *lost souls* at one point or the other. We might be aware where we are present physically, but we do not know where to go or what to do further in life.

Most of us know what we want but only a few know how to reach and the path that we take to reach our goal is what makes the difference. No matter what path we choose, we never lose hope of reaching our goal. In this marathon of life, at one point or the other, we find ourselves in the middle of nowhere. Most of us consider being lost as highly undesirable or even terrifying. We find ambiguity in whichever direction we look due to which we find ourselves to be disconnected, discouraged and disappointed. In contrary, there are people who utilize this situation to make the most out of it.

Almost everybody once in a while have found himself in this unknown territory, scared and perplexed. Something similar happened to me a few years (/months) back when I was heading to deliver the morning lecture to a batch of MBA students, something I have been doing for years now. I kissed my little daughter and headed for the nearest metro station, like always. But to my surprise, the metro rail was shut down because of some technical reasons. In my 'x'-years of teaching career there were hardly any instances when I was late for my lecture, but that day I wasn't sure whether I would even make it to the college as I never cared to discover any alternative. I was lost.

Little did I know then that this simple incident is going to manifest itself as a learning experience, that it was about to change my thinking process forever. I came out of the station and started looking for alternatives. And I discovered that there are multiple other ways to reach my destination, few are even more reliable and efficient than what I have been availing for all these years.

Did I reach my destination? Did I reach in time? Well, that's not important here, what matters is when I was forced to step out of my comfort zone, I discovered a wide array of possibilities, untapped opportunities. But like most of us, like you, I too was scared, was not willing to experiment, was not willing to move out of my comfort zone for obvious reasons, and mindlessly followed the path that was laid before me which was deemed to be the best by someone. And I immediately regretted not being lost much earlier in my life.

Indeed, the deepest form of wandering requires us to be lost. There is always light at the end of the tunnel. We can lay our own path towards success without hoping for someone to show us the path and our hope is the one which will make us walk. Unless we are lost, we cannot discover new paths to our destination. If you need to get out of the jungle, you are left with no other option but to find a way out. Hope is the one which will fuel our desire to find the way. But one thing most of us fail to realize is that only if you are lost, you can find yourself. The fun and joy of being lost is something unique. By being lost and accepting it as a reality, your life goes through a radical change. Old agendas, beliefs and desires will fade away; thoughts of new opportunities, objectives and goals will arise. The tides inside you will calm down; you will start finding serenity which will let you hear your thoughts.

This is why the Wanderer seeks to get lost.

The art of being lost is not a matter of merely getting lost, but rather being lost and enthusiastically surrendering to its unlimited potential. In fact, using it to ones advantage. The shift from being lost to being found is gradual and indirect one in a new and unpredictable way. In this course of the shift, we get to learn many new things which will give us a lot of joy. The first step to encourage this shift from being lost to found is to accept the fact that you are lost and you don't know how to reach your destination. We need to enjoy our journey towards our destination. It is not that you won't reach the destination if you do not enjoy but why missing all the fun which is on the way. At the end of the journey, we will ultimately reach our destination with some sweet memories to cherish forever.

When we are lost, we navigate the options that are available to us. And as we do so, it's possible that we will discover unexpected curves and bends on, occasionally we will even find ourselves needing to make a U-turn, but only if we dare to move forward, we will find a series of consequences and experiences that awaits us along the chosen path, new possibilities will emerge, new opportunities will surface. And therein lies the crux of the issue. Dare to be lost, to find yourself.

Life can be unfair at times. No one escapes from the audacities of life. Pain is inevitable. In between all this, what keeps us going?

Hope.

Hope serves as the lifeblood to our existence. It is a string pulling which one can open the knots of despair and misery. When you lose everything, one thing that stays with you is hope. It comes when you have no more energy to fight against the circumstances. Life gently whispers hope in our ears when we are in the direst situations reminding us that how beautiful still life is.

It forms the fifth corner of the square which is veiled yet so powerful that it forms the foundation of the four corners of the square. Without which, the other four corners of the square have no meaning. Hope is what keeps us strong, gives us courage to take chances and bring a revolution.

Keep this hope alive within you by being open to new thoughts, opportunities and welcoming life with open arms.

Hope not only provides will to reach the goal but also helps to invent different ways of reaching it. Hope gives us enormous energy at any stage of our life to reach our destination. Keep hoping.

44

A Small Tribute

When I go down the memory lane to my struggling days after I had just completed MBA, visuals of the day he gave me a book called "Who Moved My Cheese?" written by the Dr. Spencer Johnson run before my eyes.

During that phase, I was in a dilemma whether to enter into "professional marketing" or further develop my potentials.

There comes a stage in everyone's life in which one isolates himself from his/her parents. Communication between parents and children decreases. Not that one loses love for them but it is just that priorities change with time— looking after the interests and upbringings of the children, spending the whole day at work makes it difficult to find enough time to spend quality time with family. In such circumstances, my father Sri Om Prakash Jain understood that it was not feasible for me to sit at his counsel for hours every day and thus he gave me this book.

That was the turning point of the journey of my life and since then there has been no looking back. Though the book taught me how to pursue my ambitions, what principles to follow and how to groom myself; the real credit goes to my father for selecting the right things for me and thus shaping my career in a much better way.

To a great extent, today, I feel that I am a successful trainer.

Now that someone had already "moved my cheese" and with confidence jingling in my heart and mind; I was determined. Determined to enter this industry to do what I realized that I am supposed to do.

One day at the metro station, I suddenly met my school friend, Mr. Gurudutt Mishra and as expected out of two long-lost friends, we started discussing about what we studied after school where do we stand in our careers now. To my surprise he too entered this industry and was delivering his services as a teacher with sound knowledge of his subject. He asked me to come to his centre and give a demo class. That is how it began; and shortly after this I was selected as a faculty member in his institution.

One day after the class, while I was talking to him he told me about another well known personality Mr. Vishal Dhelia. Just another coincidence, this guy turned out to be my college mate. I inquired about him and met him soon and he too encouraged me to join his institution. That was the second stepping stone of my teaching career.

Gradually I moved from one centre to another and in one such centre I met Prof. Pradeep Dutta. He was the man who introduced me to M.B.A. Colleges (B-Schools) and thus I started marketing my services now to MBA pursuant and aspirants. Even today when I need his help, he makes time out of his busy schedule to talk to me and help me in the most appropriate way he can.

*　　*　　*

This book is the manifestation of a learning process that began for me over fourteen years ago. During the intervening period I come across some wonderful people in the form of relatives, friends or acquaintances from whom I have learnt immensely. While it is not possible to name them individually, I would like to express a deep sense of gratitude towards them.

This book is a way for me to continue my journey which started within four walls of a lecture room. Because time is precious, and I want to spend all that I can with my students and lectures, I asked Amita Sood for help. Each day, I spoke to Amita on my cell-phone headset. She then spent countless hours helping to turn my stories into the book that followed. My great thanks to Amita Sood for her incredible talent and professionalism.

Sincere thanks to Ms. Jyoti Ahirwar for designing the FCOC logo which features on the cover page of the book. She is a third year student of the Matoshri College of Engineering pursuing B. Tech in Information Technology. She designed around 10 logos for the book all of which were extremely impressive and choosing one amongst them became difficult for me. The best part is all of them were handmade and contained a meaningful message.

Finally, I selected one logo which best describes 'Four Corners of The Circle'.

Inspired. Amazed. Grateful. That is what Mohua Roy makes me feel for her psychological inputs when and where required.

Ms. Pooja Adhikari, Thank you for being a helping hand in creating the Salesman of the day.

I would like to acknowledge contribution made by Mr. Rohit Kant Gupta and Mr. Surajit Sengupta for drafting Opportunity of being lost.

Many thanks to Ms. Gargi Aich for preparing drafts for Talking to your Ghost.

Sincere thanks to Mr. Shaleen Dubey for proof reading and editing.

My Genuine gratitude goes to Ms. Ann Minoza, Nelson Cortez and James Clifford of Partridge Publishing, India for having faith in this book.

I would like to express my heartfelt thanks to my wonderful students. This book would not have been possible in the absence of the opportunity provided by my audiences and listeners. My sincere thanks and work of appreciation to them for being so kind and lending me their ears every now and then.

I would like to thank my colleagues who have supported me through thick and thin during the last 14 years of my

MOHIT JAIN WITH AMITA SOOD

struggle. These include Mr. Amit Sen Gupta, Mrs. Sabina Pandey and Ms. Gargi Aich.

No amount of thanks can ever repay the great debt that I owe to my family, who had provided me with the constant inspirations over the years.

To all the people who helped in making this book to last forever, just know that I think of you, I thank you and I love you.

Epilogue

A Revolution called Education

As I mentioned time and again, the real purpose of FCOC is to help its readers to grow in career aspects. One cannot achieve this growth without sustained effort and hard-work. And such hard work should have a direction. One might put in a lot of efforts but still get disappointed at the end as these efforts were not made in the right direction. For example; you sit entire day with your textbook and yet unable to comprehend a single concept at the end of the day.

Result—You know your subject, its contents but are unable to write during the examination.

Will hours of study without concentration yield any results?

Rather than this, if you study even a few concepts thoroughly, you can fetch good marks in the examination.

It is always quality that matters, quantity without quality is useless.

FCOC will teach us why such problems occur and how to tackle them.

Now think about these subjects: Production Management, Operational Management, Shop-floor data collection and training. These subjects are not much in demand in the market scenario today. They fail to attract attention as compared to other subjects. People find them boring.

An ambitious entrepreneur would always gain an extra edge over others by doing things which others fail to do. He would know what others do not know. This way he would become a master of his field.

FCOC will teach us why and how to derive interest for these subjects.

Ever did we wonder, why we still remember our nursery rhymes like Twinkle Twinkle . . . , Humpty Dumpty . . . or Little Tea Pot . . . ? Being a kid, it was surely not easy for us to learn these poems by heart.

The way our parents and teachers explained every word in detail with examples and actions, we developed a keen interest in learning them. Their teaching methodologies helped us to grasp our nursery rhymes in such a way that most of us still remember them by heart.

One must understand each concept in depth, inch by inch and line by line. That is the right way of learning.

Mugging up might help initially but eventually it might prove to be deceiving. A slip of a single word in the exam or a twist on the question makes you forget the entire answer. Thus, you will end up spoiling your exam.

Through FCOC, we have initiated a small effort to encourage trainers to follow more distinguished teaching methods. It focuses on the fact that teaching is not a business and one must not choose this profession if he only intends to make money out of it. A teacher is a salesman. He is delivering his services at the cost of customer satisfaction. Customers are his students and if they are satisfied then they will take an interest in the subject. They would learn concepts in a better and quicker way.

FCOC does not support that a trainer/teacher should not make a profit by delivering his services to his trainees/ students. It just believes that he/she is a nation-builder and should focus on the overall development of an individual.

Last but not the least, in the practical arena FCOC relates to any serviceman delivering his services to his customers/ clients. The way a service provider convinces his customers to avail his services or products depend on his marketing skills, techniques and choosing the right audience for that particular product or service.

At the same time, the customers/clients should also make the right judgement. Following the crowd or purchasing any product without doing an analysis whether the product meets their requirements is a blunder. The seller or a service provider cannot be blamed in such a situation. Self education and awareness is must for customers to be able to select the correct service, product or a career path.

A mutual trust should exist between the teacher and the student on the basis of which both of them could give the best of their potential.

Most of us are already aware of the things spoken about in this book but how many of us implement them? We somewhere inside know where we went wrong or if we are still going on a wrong track but we are unable to gain courage to correct ourselves. Only if someone pokes us, we realize that we need to mend our ways. This book is your friend and a true well wisher. It helps you to do self introspection, realize your dreams and how should to make them come true. After reading it, you would feel like taking some resolutions and would like to adhere to them.

* * *

The majority of us find text books boring. The only time we feel like studying is when exams are near. For the rest of the year, we like to watch movies, hang around with friends and gossip on phone with peers for hours.

If a teacher asks you to read an entire textbook and only then he/she would begin taking classes, would you ever read it?

Do you ever read a text book while you travel?

Even if you read it, it is only by compulsion and not by choice. The examination fear makes you read books even while you are in your school/college bus.

Now, if I give you an interesting story book or a popular novel, will you read it?

Most of us would love to read it. People who love reading will carry their novels with them wherever they go. Any time they find themselves sitting idle, they simply take out the novel from their bag and start reading it. The reason is novels are very interesting plus we can learn a lot from them.

What if even in schools and colleges, all the chapters are explained in the form of an interesting story? Learning would become simpler and students would start enjoying attending classes. No more would they yawn, dream or stay lost during the lectures. They would leave their favourite 'last benches' and sit in the front so that they do not miss even a single part of the lecture. That is my motto of providing education where learning is made fun.

J.U.I.C.E, 'Join Us In Creating Education' is our upcoming book which consists of short interesting stories guiding us how to make learning simpler. How can we bring a revolution in the education industry?

How can a small change bring a huge difference? Our motto is to join hands and make a better tomorrow. Let us improve the quality of education and help young talented minds of India make their mark in the world.

This book is not for teachers, it is not for students, it is for everyone who loves reading story books.

*   *   *

A girl child is a blessing.

She is as tender as a flower when it comes to emotions or relationships.

She is as strong as the mountains when it comes to career.

She is worthy of respect in every sense.

She is a mother, a daughter, a wife and an entrepreneur too. The world confines itself in a woman.

Our upcoming book 'To My Girl' talks about transformation of a simple girl into a diva, into an entrepreneur, ready to face the corporate world.

*   *   *

Now on juicing the Four Corners of the Circle,
I choose to become a Brand;
Local, National or International,
To be complemented wherever I stand.

To become a Brand someday,
Though the process might linger;
Though eventually an international one certainly,
That's how goes my hunger.

I motivate others
(few might be too tender)
Though knowing 'a bit' is no harm,
But what's the harm increasing your hunger?

Now the world will recognize you,
And change their way they see;
For you too have that potential match-box,
Required is just a spark of T.M.G.

*   *   *

To be successful in corporate world, one just not needs skills and talent, but also great attitude, personality and communication skills.

'Corporate Casuals' throws a light on the skills that a man must possess to survive in the corporate industry and how to shine in this industry without compromising on your dreams and principles.

So, get ready for the upcoming books, 'J.U.I.C.E', 'To My Girl' and 'Corporate Casuals' expected to release in 2014-2015.

*   *   *

The Fight! To Be Continued . . .